Royal Navy
Submarines
1901 to 2008

Royal Navy
Submarines
1901 to 2008

MAURICE COCKER

WITH DRAWINGS BY
JOHN LAMBERT

FOREWORD BY
VICE ADMIRAL SIR LANCELOT BELL DAVIES, KBE
NEW FOREWORD By
ADMIRAL SIR JAMES PEROWNE KBE

Pen & Sword
MARITIME

By the same author
Destroyers of the Royal Navy, 1893 - 1981
Observers Directory of Royal Naval Submarines 1901 - 1982
Frigates, Sloops & Patrol Vessels of the Royal Navy 1900 to date
Mine Warfare Vessels of the Royal Navy 1908 to date
West Coast Support Group TG96.8. Korea
Coastal Forces Vessels of the Royal Navy from 1865
Aircraft Carrying Ships of the Royal Navy 1912 to date

First published in Great Britain in 1982 by Frederick Warne (Publishers) Ltd, London.

Published in in 2008 under the title Royal Naval Submarines 1901 to the Present Day

and reprinted in this format by
Pen & Sword Maritime
An imprint of
Pen & Sword Books Ltd
47 Church Street
Barnsley
South Yorkshire
S70 2AS

Text Copyright © Maurice Cocker 1982, 2008
Drawings Copyright © J. Lambert 1982, 2008

ISBN 978 1 52679 190 0

The right of Maurice Cocker to be identified as Author of this work has been asserted by him in accordance with the Copyright, Designs and Patents Act 1988.

A CIP catalogue record for this book is
available from the British Library

Printed and bound in England by CPI UK

Pen & Sword Books Ltd incorporates the Imprints of Pen & Sword Aviation,
Pen & Sword Maritime, Pen & Sword Military, Wharncliffe Local History,
Pen & Sword Select, Pen & Sword Military Classics and Leo Cooper.

For a complete list of Pen & Sword titles please contact
PEN & SWORD BOOKS LIMITED
47 Church Street, Barnsley, South Yorkshire, S70 2AS, England
E-mail: enquiries@pen-and-sword.co.uk
Website: www.pen-and-sword.co.uk

This Author is a friend of the Imperial War Museum, Royal Naval Submarine Museum, Royal Naval Museum, National Maritime Museum and the Liverpool Maritime Museum and offers thanks for assistance to the Navel Historical Branch of the Ministry of Defence

CONTENTS

ACKNOWLEDGEMENTS

I am deeply indebted to the following individuals and/or Institutions, for help and advice during the compilation of this book. Additionally, I am grateful for permission to use their drawings and photographs. In random order they are:

W. K. Fox. Cammell Laird Shipbuilders, Mrs R. M. Wayman, Michell Bearings: Cdr F. E. R. Phillips, RN and Cdr F. N. Ponsonby MVO, RN, Public Relations Office, MOD (N); Lt Cdr M. R.Wilson, Naval Historical Branch MOD (N): D. W. Robinson and W. G. Clouter, Vickers Shipbuilding and Engineering Ltd.; G. Britton, Royal Navy Submarine Museum; J. Anderson, Scotts Shipbuilding Company Limited: G. B. Vaughton and D. Thornley, Manchester Ship Canal Company; Mrs G. Wilkinson, Nashua Copycat; Mrs T. Crook, Marconi Space Defence Systems Limited: M. Willis, Imperial War Museum. W. Cloots. BAE Systems. J.W. Goss.

My wife Pauline has been particulary helpful in typing the manuscript and E. F. Bunt has been of great assistance in research. If by any chance I have omitted any individual ororganization, I trust that my apology will be accepted and understood.

The general arrangement drawings have all been specially prepared by John Lambert.

Permission to reproduce the photographs is gratefully acknowledged, in particular to Vickers Shipbuilding Ltd, from whose archives all have been supplied except those noted below. Thanks are also due to Scotts Shipbuilding Lid: pages 30, 31, 41, 46; Cammell Laird Ltd: 62, 67, 94, 98, 100; Imperial War Museum: 67, 80; Ufficio Storico Marina Militare Italiana: 84, 85; Ministry of Defence (Navy): 2, 8, 10, 100, 101, 104, 105, 107, 109, 110, 111, 113, 114, 115, 121: Marconi Space and Defence Systems Ltd: 122,123; Royal Naval Submarine Museum: 19, 33, 53, 59, 83, 89, 91, 92, 93: Scott Lithgow Ltd; 40; G. Carter: 76; Fleet Air Arm Museum: 120.

Oracle preparing to enter harbour, her ship's crest and bell already in position on the conning tower. The flare of the bow is very noticeable at this angle.

Osiris

Astute

FOREWORD
by
Vice Admiral Sir Lancelot Bell Davies, KBE

The Observer's Directory of Royal Navy Submarines is published at the very moment that naval history has recorded a further significant change in naval warfare. The Falklands campaign will occupy historians for years to come. It contains many 'firsts' and many lessons. Single-ship successful actions always sparkle in the pages of history: but few mark a major turning point in naval warfare.

The sinking of the Argentine cruiser General Belgrano by HM S/M Conqueror marked such a turning point. It is the first time that a major surface combatant has been sunk by a dived submarine, capable of keeping up with its target indefinitely, and able to select the tactical moment to strike, under the operational command of a headquarters 8,000 miles away.

The immediate effect was to deny the Argentine suface naval forces any further participation in the conflict. Few single-ship actions have had such a profound strategic result.

The full story of the Royal Navy submarines' contribution to that conflict will rightly remain undisclosed for some time to come; but the impact of their presence upon the imagination of their foes goes without saying. Imagination is also the spur of the student. Any serious researcher will welcome this directory, because it provides a convenient and comprehensive catalogue of British submarines from which he can check statistical data.

But it does more than this. Anyone whose imagination is inspired by warships probably finds that browsing through an old illustrated naval reference book is a very satisfying pastime. The older the copy the better. There is something magical about the photograph of an old warship that stimulates the storyteller in us all. It matters not that the picture is a formal one, nor that the statistics are ungarnished by historical narrative—imagination thrives best without such interference.

The snag with such an old book is that it freezes time in the year of its issue. In this new directory Mr Cocker gives us the luxury of daydreaming through time as well as checking up on facts.

The advent of nuclear propulsion has provided a dramatic change to capability, and a marked improvement in the submariner's lifestyle; but the make-up of the man is the same. His courage, forebearance and tolerance of his shipmates, and his dedicated professionalism, will continue to provide food for the historian, and inspiration for the imagination of those who dream of the sea.

Thank you Mr Cocker for providing such an invaluable help to both.

Valiant Class

Porpoise

Swiftsure Class

NEW FOREWORD
by
Admiral Sir James Perowne KBE

Foreward for Royal Navy Submarines 1901 – 2008

The Observer's Directory of Royal Naval Submarines was first published in 1982 just after the Falklands War, where submarines played such a decisive part. Having owned a copy from that time, I know what a very useful and informative book this is for anyone interested in the submarine service from its inception in 1901 to the present day. I am very pleased that it has been updated to cover the last 25 years including the introduction of the Trident deterrent weapon system and the brand new Astute class the first of which is going on sea trials this year.

In 1900 the Royal Navy was slow introducing submarines in the Fleet as it recognized early the threat they posed to the might of the Battlefleets and therefore the risk to the supremacy of the Royal Navy at that time. Once they had embraced the new technology, developments moved fast and within ten years had, with the introduction of the E Class, a boat that has many of the characteristics of a modern diesel powered submarine. The young service, known at that time as "The Trade", as it was no occupation for a gentleman, acquitted itself well in the First World War and the foundations of over 100 years of success were laid. The centenary of the submarine service was celebrated in 2001 with a major update to the Royal Navy Submarine Museum at Gosport which is sited near the Alma Mater of the submariner, HMS Dolphin, now a tri-service medical establishment sadly without any submarines alongside.

As I joined submarines in 1969, the nuclear age was coming into being and a look through these pages reminds me how quickly the Royal Navy built up its nuclear fleet. In the 1960s ten nuclear powered boats were built, crews were trained and successfully went on operations in support of the Cold War, whether deterrent patrols or anti-submarine operations against the Soviet Navy. This is in addition to 15 conventional boats of the P & O class also commissioned in the 1960s; a total of 25 new submarines in 10 years. In the 25 years since this excellent book was first produced, we have built only 12 new submarines, 8 nuclear and four diesel, and those were sold some before being even commissioned. Our present numbers are too low, but I am pleased to report that the quality remains high and the Astute class should be a significant advance on any that have gone before.

I commend this most useful book.

Admiral Sir James Perowne KBE
President Submariners' Association

Narwhal

Explorer

Severn

INTRODUCTION

The purpose of this book is to fill an important gap in naval history. There has not previously been a book recording every submarine commissioned into the Royal Navy: this is an attempt to provide an illustrated directory to each one and also show the evolution of the submarine since 1901.

There are obvious difficulties in compiling a record of this type: the service histories of many of the boats (submarines are traditionally still called boats) could each fill a book. It is left to others to describe such exploits. Similarly, there are continual modifications to the design of all but the smallest Classes. While such minutiae are of interest to the specialist, they are limited here for the sake of brevity and clarity, to the more important changes.

From the Holland Class of 1901 to the Upholder Class, announced in 1979, the wheel has come full circle: the earliest submarines were powered by internal combustion engines and electric motors. Now, having gone through a cycle which has included steam turbines, both oil and nuclear driven, the latest designs are again planned to be diesel powered as were the earlier ones.

The first boats were armed with just one torpedo tube. Soon their number multiplied: guns worthy of a battleship were fitted: aircraft were carried: the submarine cruiser has armament equal to that of a frigate— though only for surface action. Today the torpedo remains the standard weapon and the heavy gun has been succeeded by the sub-surface to air and sub-surface to surface missiles. Another thing has changed—submariners have always needed stamina, but now more than ever with submarines which can it is said, stay submerged for a year.

M. P. Cocker
Cleveleys
Lancashire
2008

Repulse in the Gare Loch. The 'parrot's beak' on the fore casing contains a Sonar system.

A BRIEF ACCOUNT OF THE
SUBMARINE IN THE ROYAL NAVY

In the closing years of the nineteenth century only France could claim near-parity in sea power with Great Britain. The 'Entente Cordiale' was a decade away and France was regarded as a potential naval threat. This hazard increased by successful French attempts to build 'sousmarins'. Four such vessels were in use in the French navy by 1897, electrically powered and with compressed air reservoirs: the largest was 160ft long and displaced 266 tons.

It was not that the British were ignorant of submarine development. In 1866 Vickers had built a submarine designed by Nordenfelt, a Swedish gun-maker, for the Russian navy, but she was wrecked on her maiden voyage to St Petersburg. These craft depended on vertically mounted propellers in conjunction with ballast tanks to make them submerge. They were powered by steam engines[1] on the surface which, as was found later in the British 'K' Class, created a number of problems, including the fact that they took longer to be ready to dive than boats driven by other means.

The British Admiralty believed that its surface fleet was more than a sufficient match for such outlandish vessels and it was not considered necessary for the Royal Navy to be interested in them, though no doubt British Intelligence kept an eye on French progress.

The British attitude changed because the self-propelled torpedo provided a practical submarine weapon. In 1866 Robert Whitehead had invented this 'devil's device' which travelled beneath the water driven by compressed air. It maintained a constant depth by means of a hydrostatic valve and horizontal rudders, and Whitehead later added a servo motor and gyroscope for directional stability. The British government acquired rights to it in 1871.

In 1877 J. P. Holland, an Irish-born American immigrant,[2] applied the horizontal rudder to the submarine boats he was developing and his design was taken up by the Admiralty who placed the contract with Vickers for five Holland boats in 1900. It was the beginning of an association which has extended to the Upholder Class, announced in 1979 for building in the 1980s.

Thus it was that the 'submarine' first appeared in the Royal Navy in 1901. The first Holland boat was 63¾ x 11¾ x 10ft draught on the surface; it displaced 104 tons on the surface and 122 tons submerged. It had a single 14in torpedo tube in the bow and a surface speed of eight knots (five knots submerged). By comparison, the Holland VIII, built in the same year for the United States Navy, displaced 76 tons, but had the same surface speed.

Vickers' design staff developed changes to the Holland design and produced the Class A design which was built under the superintendence of the Admiralty. The 13 boats of this Class were followed by 11 boats in Class B in 1906 and 38 in the C Class which were completed by 1910. Displacement had now reached 290 tons on the surface and 320 tons submerged, and the armament increased to two 18in tubes. A 16cyl petrol engine provided surface power and charged the batteries for the electric motor for use when submerged. D and E Classes followed, the first Classes to depart from a purely coastal concept, and were the last to be completed before World War I. D Class had bow and stern torpedo tubes. E Class was the first also to have beam tubes

1. These early steam engines relied upon the latent heat principle and so were different from the steam turbines used in the *Swordfish* and K. Classes.
2. J. P. Holland (1840–1914) first became involved in submarine design with a view to their use against the British in the Irish fight for independence. After emigrating to America he had mixed fortune in designing boats for the US Navy and also worked for Russia and Japan.

C22 on trials.

and the first to include boats converted for minelaying. The first submarine to be mounted with a deck gun was D4, on which was fitted a single 12 pdr.

Of the World War I Classes, the small and not very successful F Class was followed by the V Class of four boats: G Class of 14 boats were the first to be fitted with a 21in stern tube in addition to four 18in tubes at the bow.

These relatively small patrol submarines were limited in their range and there was an urgent need for boats which would be capable of working with the Fleet. The first venture to this end was the *Nautilus*, built by Vickers in 1914. She was 242½ ft long and displaced 1,270 tons surfaced. Her power plant of diesel and electric motors gave her a surface speed of 17 knots (10 knots submerged). Although commissioned, she was not a success and never became operational. The experiments continued on a different tack with *Swordfish*, launched in 1916, which was powered by a steam turbine on the surface and by twin electric motors when submerged. She too suffered numerous problems and was finally converted to a surface patrol vessel at Portsmouth in 1917. The steam turbine theme was continued in the K Class, of which 18 were built. They were the fastest submarines afloat for many years, and not beaten on the surface until *Dreadnought* in 1963. They achieved a surface speed of 24 knots from twin steam turbines and also had a diesel auxiliary engine, plus twin electric motors for submerged running. A somewhat miscellaneous armament included a 3in gun or two 4in guns, machine guns and a depth charge thrower. Although designed to work with the Fleet on the surface as a scout vessel, possibly in weather too severe for a destroyer, there were many accidents culminating in two collisions in January 1918. Many of the crews were lost and the Class was phased out of service in the 1920s.

At the insistence of Commodore (S) S. S. Hall the M Class was embarked upon following the development of the German U-cruiser. Three boats were completed, each with a 12in gun. This was replaced on one with a seaplane: the other was converted for minelaying.

Other Classes of more conventional design included the H and J Classes, H Class in particular being most successful on operations, and 37 were built. The last Class of World War I was given the letter R with ten boats. Though conventional in design they were noteworthy for being nearly twice as fast submerged (15 knots) as they were on the surface (9½ knots).

After World War I the victorious powers met to reach agreement on the size of their post-war fleets. Great Britain and the USA were in favour of the abolition of submarines, but were opposed by France and Japan: Italy had reservations. It was agreed that none of the contracting powers would possess more than three boats larger than 2,000 tons displacement and that no submarine would carry a gun larger than 8in calibre. The total submarine tonnage permitted was 52,700 tons for any one of the contracting powers. Great Britain, Japan and the USA agreed to the figures.

X1, launched in 1923, was another 'one boat' experimental Class described as a 'cruiser submarine' as she carried four 5.2in guns in two turrets in addition to six 21in torpedo tubes.

The new construction programme in between the world wars produced the O, P and R Classes of 1475 tons, 1,760 tons and 1,740 tons, respectively, on the surface. They were armed with a 4in gun on a built up fore deck forward of the conning tower which enabled the ammunition to be passed up more easily and speedily. The gun was also at a higher level than before which made sighting easier and in heavy seas the crew did not have to leave the conning tower to use the gun.

There followed a design of three boats known as the Thames Class. The intention was that these should follow up the ill-fated K Class by being Fleet submarines. They displaced 2,185 tons surfaced and had a top speed of ten knots submerged. The complement of 61 was large for its time (although X1 had a planned complement of 110) and were reported to be most comfortable.

In 1931 launching of the S Class commenced with four boats of low tonnage (735 tons surfaced), built for short sea operations, with a range of 3,750 nm. The Class design was good and a second group of eight were built with a slightly larger displacement of 765 tons. As World War II neared, the third S Class group was commenced and the Class was still being launched in 1945. It reached a total of 50 boats.

The first of the Porpoise Class of six boats designed as minelayers, was launched in 1932. They carried 50 mines and were also armed with six 21in torpedo tubes in the bow and a 4in deck gun.

They were followed by the U and V Classes, originally conceived as unarmed training boats and redesigned for their armament of four 21in torpedo tubes, supplemented by a 3in gun mounted forward of the conning tower. But there was no hatch giving direct access to the gun (probably because the Class had not been designed to carry one), with the result that the conning tower became overcrowded during a gun action.

The T Class, built from 1937 to 1945 in three groups of 15, 7 and 31 boats, were of much larger tonnage (1,325 tons surfaced). They provided a very steady gun platform and a variety of torpedo tube positions. The first group had six internal and two external bow tubes, and there were a further two external tubes amidships facing forward. Later construction also included an external stern tube and the midship tubes were reversed to fire aft.

During World War II the Royal Navy was also loaned boats from the US Navy R and S Classes, vintage 1914–1918; one German U-boat was captured off Iceland and was commissioned into the Royal Navy as HMS *Graph*. Two or three Italian boats were temporarily commissioned and the Royal Navy took over, again temporarily, four boats which were being built in the UK for the Turkish Navy.

Mention must also be made of the X craft midget submarines which had many successes in attacks on heavily defended enemy harbours.

The first of the post-World War II Classes was commenced in 1943. This was the new A Class of 15 boats which continued to be built until 1948. A conversion from the original design enabled them to be fitted with the Snorkel breathing equipment, allowing fresh air to be fed to the main engines when all but the snort tubes and periscopes were submerged. These boats displaced 1,385 tons surfaced and had a submerged speed no greater than eight knots. Numbers of the A and T Classes were modernised and 'streamlined' by removal of the deck gun. Apart from those used in the Indonesian confrontation, deck armament was no longer standard equipment. They were the last of over 40 years of design with 'conventional' power systems.

The Oberon and Porpoise Classes, of 13 and 8 boats, respectively, were completed from 1958 and were an intermediate stage before the first of the nuclear-powered submarines, *Dreadnought*, which was completed in 1963. With a surface displacement of 3,500 tons, she is powered by an S5W nuclear reactor through a geared steam turbine to a single propeller. The reversion to a single screw applies to all subsequent nuclear-powered boats.

The building programme of hunter-killer nuclear-powered submarines began with the Valiant Class completed in 1966; it was followed by the Churchill Class (1970), Swiftsure Class (1974) and the Trafalgar launched in 1981, nameship of her Class.

The Upholder Class, the successor to the Oberon Class, returns to the traditional diesel power and is to a design jointly conceived by Vickers Shipbuilding and the Ministry of Defence (Navy).

In 1914, 61 boats were shown in commission. By 1918 the number had increased to 141, and at the close of World War II, 131 submarines were in commission (excluding boats captured from the enemy and being evaluated). By 1960 the figure had fallen to 53; in 1981, 30 submarines were either in commission or undergoing extensive refit.

Excalibur, which used the British development of the HTP power system.

Notes and Abbreviations

All names and numbers of boats and ships are Royal Navy designations, except where specifically stated otherwise. 'HMS' and 'HM S/M' have been omitted to avoid tedious repetition, except where necessary for clarity.

Commonwealth and Allied submarines are not included except in a few specific instances when some part of their service was with the Royal Navy.

Dimensions, tonnages and units of power are expressed in 'imperial' units – i.e. ft, tons and hp. The conversion factors for metrication are:

from feet to metres: x 0.3048

from tons to tonnes: x 1.106

A Class defines a basic design of boat. Most Classes, however, underwent modification to greater or lesser extent. Only alterations of major significance are noted.

The complement is the number of Naval personnel planned to crew the vessel.

Shaft (i.e. propeller shaft): the number of these almost invariably accords with the number of engines or motors. Mention of the number of shafts is therefore, only noted when there is a variation from the norm, or if the text is unclear.

In illustrating many of the early submarines – and as recently as those in service during the Second World War – recourse has frequently had to be made to archival material. Many of the photogaphs show signs of their age, have been copied from earlier work, or were never of the highest rank. They are included because of their intrinsic historic interest.

A COMPLETE KEY TO DETAILS IDENTIFIED ON THE GENERAL ARRANGEMENT DRAWINGS:

1.	TRIMMING TANK	17.	FUEL TANKS
2.	STEERING GEAR COMPARTMENT		(DIESEL OR PETROL)
3.	MAIN ENGINE ROOM	18.	REACTOR ROOM
4.	MAIN ENGINE	19.	RADIO ROOM
5.	MAIN MOTOR	20.	MAIN BALLAST TANK
6.	FEED WATER	21.	DIESEL ROOM
7.	TURBINE ROOM	22.	BOILER ROOM
8.	BATTERY SPACE	23.	'Q' TANK
9.	CONTROL ROOM	24.	"SNORT" MAST
10.	CREW ACCOMMODATION	25.	SEARCH PERISCOPE
11.	WARD ROOM	26.	ATTACK PERISCOPE
12.	AFTER TORPEDO TUBES	27.	W/T MAST
13.	AFTER TORPEDO STOWAGE	28.	RADAR MAST
14.	BEAM TORPEDO TUBES	29.	4-INCH GUN
15.	FORWARD TORPEDO TUBES	30.	3-INCH GUN
16.	FORWARD TORPEDO STOWAGE	31.	SONAR ROOM

THE FOLLOWING ABREVIATIONS HAVE BEEN EMPLOYED THROUGHOUT THE BOOK

AA	anti-aircraft		MTB	motor torpedo boat
A/S	anti-submarine		mtg	mounting for gun
bp	between perpendiculars		MV	motor vessel
bhp	brake horsepower		nm	nautical mile
DP	dual purpose		pdr	pounder (weight of gun projectile)
E-boat	high speed German patrol boat		shp	shaft horse power
HA	high angle		SS	steam ship
HE	high explosive		TB	torpedo boat (Italian)
LA	low angle		tubes	torpedo tubes
MA/SB	motor anti-submarine boat		wl	waterline (length)
mg	machine gun		WT	wireless telegraph
M/S	minesweeper			

Photo of restored Holland S/M at the Royal Naval S/M Museum.

	launched	builder
No 1	1901	All boats were built by
No 2–5	1902	Vickers Son & Maxim
Completion:	1901–3	

Specification

Displacement	surfaced:	104 tons
	submerged:	*No 1* 122 tons
		Nos 2–5 150 tons
Dimensions:		63¾ x 11¾ x 10 ft
Complement:		7
Propulsion	surfaced:	Single 4 cyl petrol engine;
		No 1 160 hp, *Nos 2–5* 250 hp
	submerged:	Single electric motor 74 hp
Speed	surfaced:	8 knots
	submerged:	5 knots
Range:		500 nm
Armament	Gun:	see armament note
	Torpedo:	Single 14 in bow tube

Class note: With this new branch of the Service and a new type of vessel there were numerous teething troubles, but by determination and trial and error the crews became accustomed to their boats and efficiency constantly improved. In exercises, many a captain of a super-Dreadnought was exceedingly surprised to find that a 'torpedo' had struck his ship without him even having been aware that a submarine was in the offing.

The Class was completed without periscopes; Capt R. Bacon, RN, devised a vertical telescope which fulfilled the purpose.

As trials continued and from constant use, ideas for improvement influenced the design of the A Class.

In the same period the USN Adder Class, also designed by Holland, had a range of 800 nm.

No 4 was used as gunnery target on 17 October 1912.

No 5 was lost while under tow on 8 August 1912.

None of the Class remained in service by 1913.

Armament note: The Class was designed to have an 8 in 'aerial gun' at the bow above the torpedo tube. The gun was to be 11¼ ft long, with a range of 1 mile, and fire a 22 Ib projectile from a 100 Ib gun-cotton charge. There is no evidence that it was fitted.

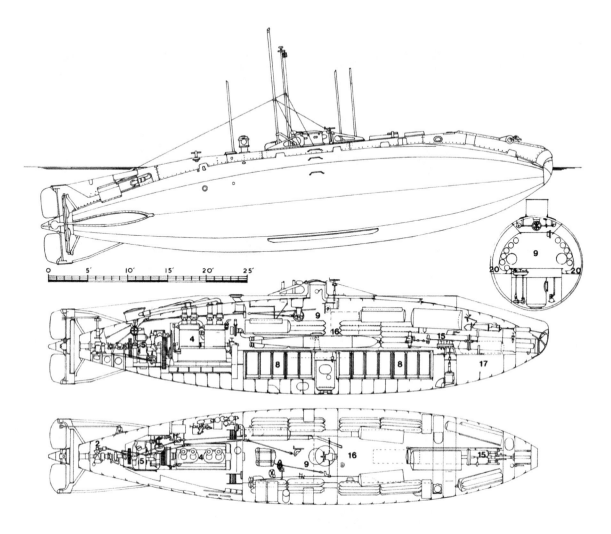

2 STEERING GEAR COMPARTMENT
4 MAIN ENGINE
5 MAIN MOTOR
8 BATTERY SPACE
9 CONTROL ROOM

15 FORWARD TORPEDO TUBE
16 TORPEDO STOWAGE
17 FUEL TANK
20 MAIN BALLAST TANK

Historical note: Submarine number 1 of this Class which had foundered whilst in tow to the Breakers yard has now been raised from the sea bed and is on display at the Royal Naval Submarine Museum, Portsmouth.

A posed photograph of Holland No 2 running on the surface, with her crew in their best shore-going rig.

A4 on builder's trials. Note the inch gauge on the bow, to aid trimming, and the rig of the crew.

	launched	*builder*
A1	1902	The complete Class
A2–A4	1903	was built by Vickers at
A5–A6	1904	Barrow-in-Furness
A7–A13	1905	
A14 became *B1*		
Completion:	1903–5	

Specification

Displacement	surfaced:	*A1–A4* 165 tons
		A5–A14 180 tons
	submerged:	*A1–A4* 180 tons
		A5–A14 207 tons
Dimensions:		*A1–A4* 100 x 11½ x 11½ ft
		A5–A14 99 x 12½ x 12½ ft
Complement:		11–14
Propulsion	surfaced:	*A1–A4* single 12 cyl petrol engine 500 hp
		A5–A12 and *A14* single 16 cyl petrol engine 550 hp
		A13 single heavy oil engine
	submerged:	*A1–A14* single electric motor 150 hp
Speed	surfaced:	11 knots (*A13* 10 knots; range 310 miles)
	submerged:	7 knots
Armament	Torpedo:	*A1* single 18 in bow tube
		A2–A14 two 18 in bow tubes

Class note: This was the first Admiralty-designed submarine. It was the first Class to have a conning tower (not included in the Holland Class), which was of great advantage in navigation, ship handling and pilotage, and gave increased visibility when the boat was on the surface.

Losses

A1 was the first Royal Navy submarine to be lost in peace or war. She sank after collision with SS *Berwick Castle* on 18 March 1904; she was salvaged and recommissioned but again sank, with further loss of life, while on trials in August 1911.

A2 foundered after grounding in Bomb Ketch Lake, Portsmouth, in January 1920.

A3 sank after collision with HMS *Hazard* on 2 February 1912. She was raised and used as a target, finally sinking in May 1912.

A4 sank after a collision in harbour at Devonport in 1905.

A7 dived into the mud and was trapped in White Sand Bay on 16 January 1914.

A8 sank in Plymouth Sound on 8 June 1905, but was salvaged.

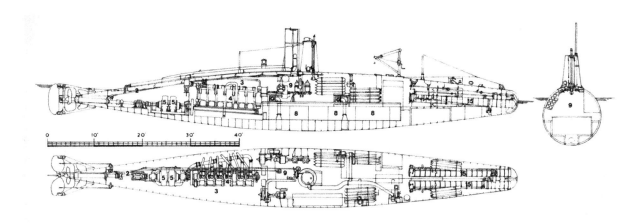

2 STEERING GEAR COMPARTMENT
3 MAIN ENGINE ROOM
4 MAIN ENGINE
5 MAIN MOTOR

8 BATTERY SPACE
9 CONTROL ROOM
15 FORWARD TORPEDO TUBE

A1. The canvas dodgers are missing from the conning tower, aft of which the compass binnacle can be seen below and behind the 'scaffolding' lookout position.

23

B4 on builder's trails. Note the ventilator on the conning tower.

	launched	builder
B1 (ex A14)	1904	The complete Class
B2–B7	1905	was built by Vickers
B8–B11	1906	at Barrow-in-Furness
Completion:	1905–6	

Class note: This Class was the first Royal Navy submarine to be fitted with forward hydroplanes.

In the latter part of World War I, B6, B7, B8, B9 and B11 were extensively modified for surface use as patrol boats. The electric motor and conning tower were removed, the deck level raised and a wheelhouse added. They were re-designated S6—S10 and saw service in the Mediterranean.

Specification

Displacement	surfaced:	280 tons
	submerged:	313 tons
Dimensions:		135 x 13½ x 12 ft
Complement:		16
Propulsion	surfaced:	Single 16 cyl petrol engine 600 hp
	submerged:	Single electric motor 180 hp Fuel capacity 15 tons
Speed	surfaced:	13 knots
	submerged:	8 knots
Range	surfaced:	1000 nm at 8½ knots
Armament	Torpedo:	Two 18 in bow tubes

Losses

B2 was sunk in collision in the Strait of Dover by SS *Amerika* on 14 October 1912.

B10 was destroyed by bombing while under repair in Venice dockyard on 9 August 1916.

B1 leaving harbour with the casing party on the conning tower and the periscope raised.

The launch of C3. Note the forward hydroplanes and the riveting round the lower bow and the bilge keels.

	launched	builder
C1–C6	1906	
C7–C12	1907	C1–C16
C13	1908	Vickers,
C14	1907	Barrow-in-Furness
C15, C16	1908	
C17–C20	1908	HM Dockyard Chatham
C21–C24	1908	Vickers,
C25–C32	1909	Barrow-in-Furness
C33, C34	1909	HM Dockyard Chatham
C35, C36	1909	Vickers,
C37, C38	1910	Barrow-in-Furness
Completion:	1906-10	

Specification

Displacement	surfaced:	290 tons
	submerged:	320 tons
Dimensions:		135 x 13½ x 12 ft
Complement:		16
Propulsion	surfaced:	Single 16 cyl petrol engine 600 hp
	submerged:	Single electric motor 200 hp
Speed	surfaced:	13 knots
	submerged:	8 knots
Range	surfaced:	1500 nm at 8½ knots
Armament	Torpedo:	Two 18 in bow tubes

Class note: As they came to be refitted, the Class was fitted with W/T. The periscopes were increased in length and two were fitted.

Losses

C3 was used to blow up the Mole at Zeebrugge on 23 April 1918.*

C11 was in collision with SS *Eddystone* off Cromer on 14 July 1909.

C14 was in collision with Hopper No 29 in Plymouth Sound on 10 December 1913. She was salvaged.

C26 and *C27* were scuttled in Helsingfors Bay on 4 April 1918.+

C29 was mined in the North Sea on 29 August 1915.

C31 foundered, cause unknown, off the Belgian coast on 4 January 1915.

C32 went aground in the Gulf of Riga on 24 October 1917 and was destroyed by own forces.

C33 failed to return from patrol in the North Sea and is believed to have been lost on 4 August 1915.

C34 was torpedoed by *U-52* off the Shetland Isles on 21 July 1917.

C35 was scuttled in Helsingfors Bay on 5 April 1918.+

*C3's bows were filled with explosive with which she rammed the Mole. Her Captain was awarded the VC.

+The loss of these three boats and four of the E Class was a result of the German—Russian armistice in December 1917 and the Peace Treaty between Germany and Finland on 7 March 1918, which required that the British Baltic submarine flotilla should be handed over to the Germans. The flotilla had been very successful in sinking German shipping carrying Swedish iron ore for the German war machine. To avoid this surrender the Commanding Officer arranged that all his boats should be scuttled and their crews brought ashore.

D6 running on the surface, the watch in their white submarine jerseys indulging in semaphore practice.

	launched	builder
D1	1908	Vickers, Barrow-in-Furness
D2–D4	1910	Vickers, Barrow-in-Furness
D5	1911	Vickers, Barrow-in-Furness
D6	1912	Vickers, Barrow-in-Furness
D7, D8	1912	HM Dockyard, Chatham

Specification from D1

Displacement	surfaced:	550 tons
	submerged:	595 tons
Dimensions:		162 x 20½ x 14 ft
Complement:		25
Propulsion	surfaced:	Single petrol engine 565 hp
	submerged:	Single electric motor 275 hp
Speed	surfaced:	16 knots
	submerged:	9 knots
Range	surfaced:	2,500 nm at 10 knots
Armament	Torpedo:	Three 18 in tubes, two bow, one stern

Specification from D2 to D8

Displacement	surfaced:	604 tons
	submerged:	620 tons
Dimensions:		162 x 20½ x 14 ft
Complement:		25
Propulsion	surfaced:	Two diesel engines 1200 hp
	submerged:	Two electric motors 550 hp
Speed	surfaced:	16 knots
	submerged:	9 knots
Range	surfaced:	2,500 nm at 10 knots
Armament	Gun:	D4 Single 4 in (see armament note); D5–D8 were fitted with one or two 12 pdrs when they were refitted
	Torpedo:	Three 18 in tubes, two bow, one stern

Note: D1 had a petrol engine, the rest of the Class had diesel engine's.

D6 cruising, her pennant number prominent.

Class note: This Class incorporated saddle tanks in lieu of internal ballast tanks. The conning tower was larger than any previous Class. They were the first boats designed to incorporate a W/T system, though the wireless mast had to be raised and lowered by hand.

During Fleet manoeuvers in 1910, *D1* successfully 'torpedoed' two 'enemy' cruisers–an augury of events in the coming war.

Armament note: This Class was the first to be armed on deck. D4 had one 12 pdr mounted in a housing which could be retracted into the conning tower, using compressed air. No shell magazine was fitted.

Losses
D1 was sunk in target practice on 23 October 1918.
D2 was sunk by gunfire from a German patrol vessel off the Ems Estuary on 25 November 1914.
D3 sank after being bombed in error by a French airship on 15 March 1918.
D5 was mined off Great Yarmouth on 3 November 1914.
D6 was torpedoed by UB-73 off the coast of Ulster on 28 June 1918.

The launch of D1 at Barrow-in-Furness.

E20 in harbour with the majority of her crew. Note the draught marks on the saddle tank, a miniature boat boom on the side of the casing, and the gun partially elevated.

1 TRIMMING TANK	10 CREW ACCOMMODATION
2 STEERING GEAR COMPARTMENT	11 WARD ROOM
3 MAIN ENGINE ROOM	12 ATFER TORPEDO TUBES
4 MAIN ENGINE	13 AFTER TORPEDO STOWAGE
5 MAIN MOTOR	14 BEAM TORPEDO TUBES
8 BATTERY SPACE	15 FORWARD TORPEDO TUBES
9 CONTROL ROOM	16 FORWARD TORPEDO STOWAGE
	17 FUEL TANKS

	launched	builder
Group 1		
E1, E2	1912	HM Dockyard, Chatham
(exD9, D10)		
E3–E6	1912	Vickers,
		Barrow-in-Furness
Completion	1913	

Specification

Displacement	surfaced:	660 tons
	submerged:	810 tons
Dimensions:		176 bp x 22½ x 12 ft
Complement:		30
Propulsion	surfaced:	Two diesel engines 1,600 hp
	submerged:	Two electric motors 840 hp
		Fuel capacity 45 tons
Speed	surfaced:	16 knots
	submerged:	10 knots
Range	surfaced:	2,500 nm at 10 knots
Armament	Gun:	Single 6 pdr or 4 in
		(see armament note)
	Torpedo:	Four 18 in, two bow, two
		beam (see armament note)

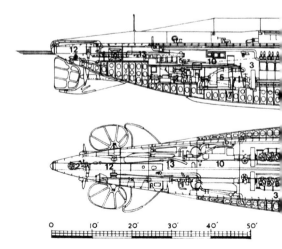

	launched	builder
Group 2		
E7, E8	1912	HM Dockyard, Chatham
E9, E10	1913	Vickers, Barrow-in-Furness
E11	1914	Vickers, Barrow-in-Furness
E12–E13	1913	HM Dockyard, Chatham
E14–E16	1914	Vickers, Barrow-in-Furness
E17–E21	1915	Vickers, Barrow-in-Furness

	launched	builder
Group 3		
E22–E24	1915	Vickers, Barrow-in-Furness
E25	1915	Beardmore
E26	1916	Beardmore
E27	1916	Yarrow
E29, E30	1916	Armstrong
E31	1916	Scotts
E32	1916	White
E33, E34	1916	Thornycroft
E35, E36	1916	John Brown
E37, E38	1916	Fairfield
E39, E40	1916	Palmer
E41, E42	1915	Cammell Laird
E43, E44	1916	Swan Hunter
E45, E46	1916	Cammell Laird
E47	1916	Fairfield (completed by Beardmore)
E48	1917	Fairfield (completed by Beardmore)
E49	1917	Swan Hunter
E50	1917	John Brown
E51	1916	Scotts
E52	1917	Denny
E53	1916	Beardmore
E54	1917	Beardmore
E55, E56	1917	Denny
Completion	1913–17	

Specification as Group 1 except:

Displacement	surfaced:	662 tons
	submerged:	835 tons
Dimensions:		181 x 23½ x 12½ ft
Armament		E7 and E8 as Group 1; E9 onwards:
	Torpedo:	Five 18 in tubes, two bow, two beam, one stern (see armament note)
	Mines:	E24, E34, E41, E45, E46, E51 were converted for minelaying. The beam tubes were omitted and they had capacity for 20 mines

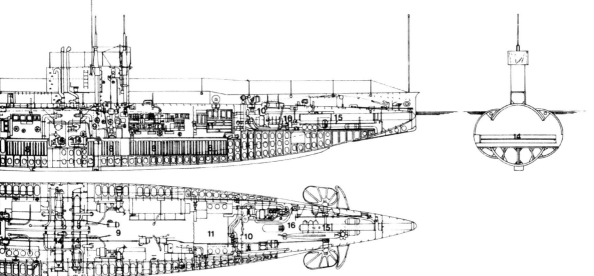

29

Class note: *E28* was cancelled. *E25* and *E26* were ordered by the Turkish Government, but were retained by the Royal Navy.

Armament note: From the E Class onwards all submarines were built with one or more magazines for gun ammunition. No standard weapon had been decided upon. For example, *E19* had one 2 pdr; *E20* had a 6 in howitzer; *E21* had both a 12 and a 2 pdr, the latter being portable and stowed inside the boat; *E11* had one 6 pdr, and *E12* a single 4 in gun.

Losses

E4 and *E41* were in collision off Harwich on 15 August 1916. *E4* was submerged and *E41* cruising on the surface when the accident occurred; there was great loss of life. Both boats were salvaged, recommissioned in May 1917, and continued in service for the remainder of the war.

E1, E8, E9 and *E19* were scuttled in Helsingfors Bay on 3–4 April 1918. See footnote, p. 25

E3 was lost on 18 October 1914. One account states that she was torpedoed by *U-27* in the North Sea; another that she was sunk by SMS *Strassburg* in the Heligoland Bight.

E5 was lost, reason unknown, in the North Sea on or after 7 March 1916.

E6 was mined on 26 December 1915 in the North Sea.

E7 was blown up by Turkish forces after becoming trapped in anti-submarine nets in the Dardanelles.

E6 outward bound on a glassy sea showing the resistance created by this form of bow. The saddle tanks are visible below the aft of the conning tower due to the speed of the boat.

E10 was lost, cause unknown, in the North Sea on or after 18 January 1915.

E13 was interned by the Danish authorities on 18 August 1915 after running aground at Saltholm while under fire from German destroyers.

E14 was mined in the Dardanelles on 22 January 1918.

E15 ran aground at Kephez Point in the Dardanelles on 15 April 1915. To avoid capture by the Turks she was torpedoed by picket boats from HMS *Majestic* and *Triumph*.

E16 was mined off the Heligoland Bight on 22 August 1916.

E17 ran aground and was wrecked in the Texel estuary on 6 January 1916.

E18 was sunk in a surface action on 24 May 1916 with SMS 'K' (the equivalent of a British 'Q ship') in the Baltic.

E20 was torpedoed by *UB-15* in the Sea of Marmara on 5 November 1915.*

E22 was torpedoed by *UB-18* in the North Sea on 25 April 1916.

E24 was mined in the North Sea on 24 March 1916.

E26 was lost, reason unknown, in the North Sea on 6 July 1916.

F2 running on the surface with both periscopes raised. The radio aerial is the long wire used on submarines until the 1950s.

E30 was lost, reason unknown, in the North Sea on or after 22 November 1916.

E34 was mined in the North Sea on 20 July 1918.

E36 was lost, reason unknown, in the North Sea on or after 17 January 1917.

E37 was lost, reason unknown, in the North Sea on or after 1 December 1916.

E47 was lost, reason unknown, in the North Sea on or after 20 August, 1917.

E49 was mined and sank off the Shetlands on 12 March 1917.

E50 was mined and sank in the North Sea on 1 February 1918.

*The loss of E20 was an unfortunate example of Anglo–French co-operation during World War 1. E20 was to have rendezvoused with the French submarine *Turquoise* for a joint patrol in the Bosphorus, but she ran aground and surrendered to the Turkish naval forces. Her CO made no attempt to destroy his confidential books and signals, which the Germans acquired and of which they took full advantage. In consequence *UB–15* was waiting for E20 and torpedoed her.

F Class

	launched	builder
F1	1914	HM Dockyard, Chatham
F2	1914	White
F3	1915	Thornycroft

Cancellations: F4–58 were projected but cancelled.

Completion   1915–17

Specification

Displacement	surfaced:	353 tons
	submerged:	525 tons
Dimensions:		151 x 16 x 10½ ft
Complement:		18–20
Propulsion	surfaced:	Two diesel engines 900 hp
	submerged:	Two electric motors 400 hp
Speed	surfaced:	14½ knots
	submerged:	9 knots
Range	surfaced:	3,000 nm at 9 knots
		Fuel capacity: 17½ tons
Armament	Gun:	Single 2 pdr
	Torpedo:	Three 18 in tubes, two bow, one stern

Note: The boats of this Class were an Admiralty design for a coastal submarine and it is not surprising that the lead boat, F1, was built at HM Dockyard, Chatham.

Rumour prevails that the Fs were based on the Vickers 'V design for a coastal boat but design improvements included a stern torpedo tube, larger hydroplanes and more effective plane guards.

The 'F' boats were found to be less buoyant than the 'V' but all in all were quite comparable. Both Classes were fitted with self-compensating fuel tanks.

There were no war losses.

	launched	builder
V1	1914	Vickers, Barrow-in-Furness
V2–V4	1915	Vickers, Barrow-in-Furness
Completion:	1914–16	

Specification

Displacement	surfaced:	364 tons
	submerged:	486 tons
Dimensions:		148 x 16 x 11 ft
Complement:		18
Propsulion	surfaced:	Two diesel engines 900 hp
	submerged:	Two electric motors 380 hp
Speed	surfaced:	14 knots
	submerged:	9 knots
Range	surfaced:	3,000 nm at 9 knots
Armament	Gun:	Single 6 pdr
	Torpedo:	Two 18 in tubes, bow only

Class note: In extremis it was not unknown for the CO of a submarine needing extra speed to connect the electric motors as well as the diesels to the shafts whilst on the surface. This could be done for a comparatively short time as, with both methods of propulsion in use, the batteries quickly lost their charge and the diesels were not able to recharge them.

V3 on basin trials with a canvas dodger which appears to have been tailored to fit.

1 TRIMMING TANK	10 CREW ACCOMMODATION
2 STEERING GEAR COMPARTMENT	15 FORWARD TORPEDO TUBES
3 MAIN ENGINE ROOM	16 FORWARD TORPEDO STOWAGE
4 MAIN ENGINE	17 FUEL TANKS
5 MAIN MOTOR	20 MAIN BALLAST TANK
8 BATTERY SPACE	25 SEARCH PERISCOPE
9 CONTROL ROOM	26 ATTACK PERISCOPE
	27 W/T MAST

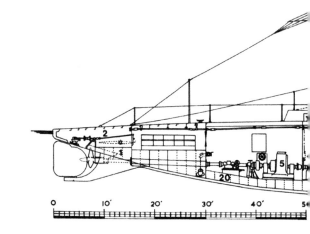

V1 at her mooring in the dockyard after commissioning. The plethora of radio aerials is extraordinary, as also are the safety rails. These were presumably fitted for basin trials as it is doubtful if she would go to sea with so much 'fencing' to create resistance.

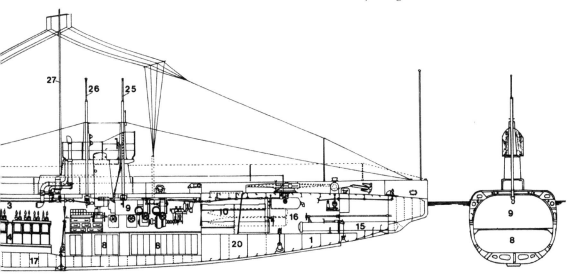

	launched	builder
S1, S2	1914	Scotts

An S Class boat built in the UK for the Italian Navy. The boat, although looking a little woe begone, is on trials in the Clyde.

Specification

Displacement	surfaced:	265 tons
	submerged:	324 tons
Dimensions:		148½ x 14 x 9½ ft
Complement:		18–21
Propulsion	surfaced:	Two diesel engines 600 hp
	submerged:	Electric motors 400 hp
		Two shafts
Range	surfaced:	1,600 nm at 8½ knots
	submerged:	75 nm at 5½ knots
Armament	Gun:	Single quick-firing
	Torpedo:	Two 18 in bow tubes

Class note: This Class was also known as the Scott-Laurenti type. They were built to an Italian design, for whose navy they were originally intended. They were commissioned into the Royal Navy and served with the 4th and 8th submarine flotillas until October 1915. S3, from the same builder, was launched in 1915 but not commissioned into the Royal Navy. All three boats were then passed over to the Italian Navy.

S1 in dry dock at Scotts yard, presumably after trials. The flat stern appears to have been renewed.

	launched	*builder*
W1	1914	Armstrong
W2–W4	1915	Armstrong

Specification

Displacement	surfaced:	*W1*, *W2* 331 tons
		W3, *W4* 320 tons
	submerged:	*W1*, *W2* 499 tons
		W3, *W4* 490 tons
Dimensions:		*W1*, *W2* 171½ x 15½ x 9 ft
		W3, *W4* 149½ x 17 x 9½ ft
Complement:		19
Propulsion	surfaced:	*W1*, *W2* two diesel engines 750 hp
		W3, *W4* two diesel engines 700 hp
	submerged:	Two electric motors 480 hp
Speed	surfaced:	13 knots
	submerged:	8 knots
Range	surfaced:	2,500 nm at 8 knots
	submerged:	65 nm at 5 knots
Armament	Gun:	Single 3 in
	Torpedo:	Two 18 in tubes (see armament note)

W4, probably entering harbour. She is wearimg the Royal Italian Navy ensign.

Class note: The Class was known as the Armstrong-Laubeuf type, having been built in the UK for the Italian Navy. *W1* and *W2* were commissioned into the Royal Navy and served in the 10th submarine flotilla until *W3* and *W4* were completed in August 1916. All four were then transferred to the Italian Navy.

Armament note: *W1* and *W2* were fitted with four torpedo tubes, two on each beam. They were angled forward on 'drop frames' fitted to the external casing below the water line.

	launched	builder
G1	1914	HM Dockyard, Chatham
G2–G5	1915	HM Dockyard, Chatham
G6, G7	1915	Armstrong
G8–G13	1916	Vickers
G14	1916	Scotts
Completion	1915–17	

Specification

Displacement	surfaced:	700 tons
	submerged:	975 tons
Dimensions:		187 x 22½ x 13½ ft
Complement:		31
Propulsion	surfaced:	Two diesel engines 1,600 hp
	submerged:	Two electric motors 840 hp
		Fuel capacity 44 tons
Speed	surfaced:	14½ knots
	submerged:	10 knots
Range	surfaced:	2,400 nm at 12 knots
Armament	Gun:	Single 3 in
		(see armament note)
	Torpedo:	Four 18 in tubes, two bow, two beam
		One 21 in stern tube

G8 in commission with enhanced armament of a 3 pdr gun aft of the conning tower

Armament note: These were the first Royal Naval submarines to be armed with the 21 in torpedo. The Class was normally intended to carry one 12 pdr and one 2 pdr portable gun.

Losses

G7 was lost due to enemy action on 1 November 1918 in the North Sea.

G8 was lost on 14 January 1918, or thereafter, in the North Sea, reason unknown.

G9 was attacked on 16 September 1917 and sunk in error by HMS *Petard* off the Norwegian coast.

G11 ran aground and was wrecked while entering Harwich harbour on 22 November 1918.

G10 on the surface with her radio masts vertical, duty watch on the conning tower and a canvas cover on the breech of her 3 in gun.

	launched	*builder*
Nautilus	1914	Vickers,
		Barrow-in-Furness
Completed:	1917	

1 TRIMMING TANK
2 STEERING GEAR COMPARTMENT
3 MAIN ENGINE ROOM
4 MAIN ENGINE
5 MAIN MOTOR
8 BATTERY SPACE
9 CONTROL ROOM
10 CREW ACCOMMODATION
11 WARD ROOM
12 AFTER TORPEDO TUBES
13 AFTER TORPEDO STOWAGE
14 BEAM TORPEDO TUBES
15 FORWARD TORPEDO TUBES
16 FORWARD TORPEDO STOWAGE
17 FUEL TANKS
20 MAIN BALLAST TANK

Specification

Displacement	surfaced:	1,270 tons
	submerged:	1,694 tons
Dimensions:		242½ x 26 x 16 ft
Propulsion	surfaced:	Two diesel engines 3,700 hp
	submerged:	Two electric motors 1,000 hp
Speed	surfaced:	17 knots
	submerged:	10 knots
Range	surfaced:	5,000 nm at 10 knots
Armament	Gun:	Single 12 pdr (one 3 in DP /
		HA gun on commissioning)
	Torpedo:	Six 18 in bow tubes

Class notes: This experimental boat was designed for long-range use. It suffered many teething troubles and did not become operational.

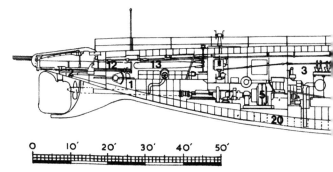

Nautilus edging past the floating dry dock on the left, in which can be seen a submarine hull, probably of an E Class boat.

HM S/M Nautilus was a 'one off design for an ocean going submarine. She was built with a double hull but was slower than expected.

Nautilus was ordered early in 1913, and not completed until late 1917. The Admiralty instructed that work was to be stopped on her (due to the delays with her engines) to permit work to be carried out on more urgent submarine construction.

Commodore(S) in 1914 had reported 'Nautilus is regarded as an exceedingly interesting experiment, and on the results of her trials depends very largely the future of the large submarine in the British Navy ...'

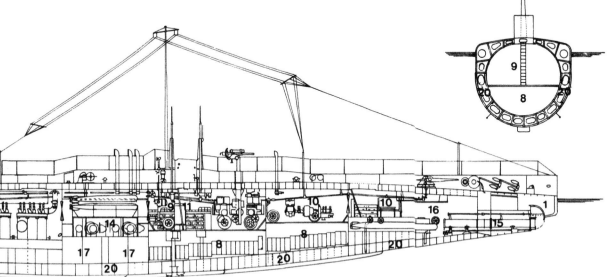

	launched	builder
Group 1		
H1–H10	1915	Canadian Vickers
H11, H12*	1917	Fore River Plant, Quincy, Mass, USA

A Group 2 boat of H Class leaving for trials after commissioning.

Specification

Displacement	surfaced:	364 tons
	submerged:	434 tons
Dimensions:		150 x 15½ x 12½ ft
Propulsion	surfaced:	Two diesel engines 480 hp
	submerged:	Two electric motors 320 hp
		Fuel capacity 16 tons
Speed	surfaced:	13 knots
	submerged:	11 knots
Armament	Torpedo:	Four 18 in bow tubes

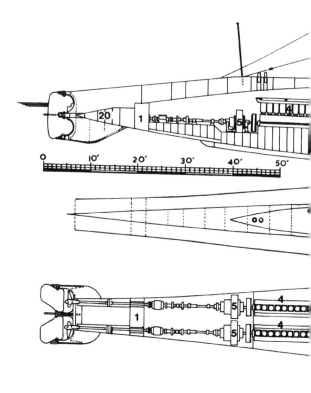

	launched	builder
Group 2		
H21, H22	1917	Vickers
H23	1918	Vickers
H24	1917	Vickers
H25	1918	Vickers
H26	1917	Vickers
H27–H32	1918	Vickers
H33, H34	1918	Cammell Laird
H41, H42	1918	Armstrong
H43, H44	1919	Armstrong
H47	1918	Beardmore
H48–H50	1919	Beardmore
H51	1918	HM Dockyard, Pembroke
H52	1919	HM Dockyard, Pembroke

Cancellations: The following boats were cancelled in
1917: *H35–40* (Cammell Laird); *H45, H46* (Armstrong);
H53, H54 (HM Dockyard, Devonport).

Specification

Displacement	surfaced:	440 tons
	submerged:	500 tons
Dimensions:		171 x 15½ x 14 ft
Complement:		22
Propulsion :		As Group 1
Speed:		As Group 1
Range	surfaced:	1,600 nm at 10 knots
Armament	Gun:	Single 12 pdr
		(some boats only)
	Torpedo:	Four 21 in bow tubes

*These two boats were not delivered until the United
States entered the war. H15–H20 were built but not
delivered.*

1 TRIMMING TANK
3 MAIN ENGINE ROOM
4 MAIN ENGINE
5 MAIN MOTOR
8 BATTERY SPACE
9 CONTROL ROOM
10 CREW ACCOMMODATION
11 WARD ROOM

15 FORWARD TORPEDO TUBES
16 FORWARD TORPEDO STOWAGE
17 FUEL TANKS
19 RADIO ROOM
20 MAIN BALLAST TANK
25 SEARCH PERISCOPE
26 ATTACK PERISCOPE
27 RADIO MAST

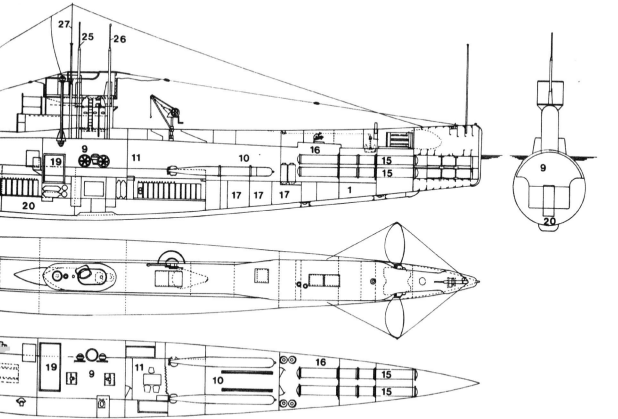

Losses

H3 was mined off Cattaro in the Adriatic Sea on 15 July 1916.

H4 foundered in the English Channel on 3 September 1913. She was salvaged and used as a target in the following year.

H5 was lost in collision in the Irish Sea on 6 March 1918.

H6 was interned by the Netherlands Navy on 8 January 1916 after stranding on Schiermonnikoog. In February 1916 she was salvaged and purchased by the Netherlands Navy who commissioned her as *08*. In 1940, as a result of the German occupation of Holland, she was scuttled at Dan Helder but again salvaged and commissioned into the German navy as *UD1*. She served as an operational U-boat until March 1943. On 3 May 1945 she was scuttled for the second time and later broken up at Kiel.

H10 was lost, reason unknown, on or after 19 January 1918 in the North Sea.

H29 sank in Devonport dockyard in August 1926.

H31 was mined in the Bay of Biscay on 24 December 1941.

H42 sank after a collision with the destroyer HMS *Versatile* off Gibraltar on 23 March 1922.

H47 sank after collision with *L12* off the Welsh coast on 9 July 1929.

H49 was torpedoed by German E-boats off the Dutch coast on 27 October 1940.

H42 with the casing party manoeuvring a torpedo for stowage below.

	launched	builder
J1, J2	1915	HM Dockyard, Portsmouth
J3 (exJ7)	1915	HM Dockyard, Pembroke
J4 (exJ8)	1916	HM Dockyard, Pembroke
J5, J6	1915	HM Dockyard, Devenport
J7	1917	HM Dockyard, Devenport

Specification

Displacement	surfaced:	1,210 tons (J7 1,260 tons)
	submerged:	1,820 tons (J7 1,826 tons)
Dimensions:		275½ x 23 x 16 ft
Complement:		44
Propulsion	surfaced:	Three diesel engines 3,600 hp
	submerged:	Three electric motors 1,400 hp, Fuel capacity 80 tons
Speed:	surfaced:	19½ knots
	submerged:	9½ knots
Range	surfaced:	5,000 nm at 12½ knots
Armament	Gun:	One or two 3 or 4 in mounted at the same level as the conning tower but on separate platform (see armament note)
	Torpedo:	Six 18 in tubes; four bow, two beam

J5 entering harbour. Note the 3 in gun at full depression, and the forward hydroplane in its recess.

Class note: Boats of this Class were the forerunners of the K Class, but diesel powered. It will be noticed from the photograph that the bow shape is similar.

Armament note: As designed, J Class submarines had one 3 in DP/HA and one 2 pdr portable gun, but a 4 in gun was mounted on some of the Class.

Loss

J6 was mistaken for a U-boat and sunk by gunfire by the 'Q' ship *Cymric* off BIyth, Northumberland, on 15 October 1918.

	launched	builder
Swordfish	1916	Scotts

(later *S1*, then again *Swordfish*)

Specification

Displacement	surfaced:	932 tons
	submerged:	1,470 tons
Dimensions:		231¼ x 23 x 14½ ft
Propulsion	surfaced:	Steam turbine 3,750 hp
	submerged:	Two electric motors 1,400 hp
		Two shafts
Speed:	surfaced:	18 knots
	submerged:	10 knots
Armament	Gun:	Nil (see armament note)
	Torpedo:	Two 21 in and four 18 in tubes

Armament note: *Swordfish* was designed to have two 3 in DP/HA guns on single disappearing mountings.

Note: This experimental steam turbine powered submarine, the predecessor of the K Class, was a further development of the diesel powered J Class (which was faster on the surface than *Swordfish*) in the attempt to find an ideal design for a fleet, as distinct from a patrol, submarine.

The Admiralty intended then, and the theory still lingers, that submarines should form an integral part of the battle fleet. Therefore they had to have the speed to keep up with the surface ships. Even on the surface that was difficult, and there was the added hazard that submarines, because of their size and low profile, were vulnerable to collision damage.

Swordfish was not a success and, after various trials, she was refitted as a surface patrol vessel. The major modifications were to remove the electric motors, add sheer to her bows to aid seaworthiness, and a wheelhouse. She was armed with two 12 pdr guns and served the rest of her short career creditably at Portsmouth.

Swordfish with a 'bone in her teeth' as she makes speed, and smoke, on trials.

Swordfish on trials. Compare the hull shape with the Italian S Class.

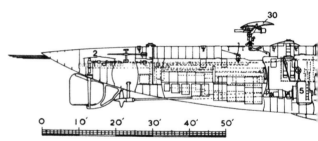

2 STEERING GEAR COMPARTMENT
4 MAIN ENGINE
5 MAIN MOTOR
6 FEED WATER
7 TURBINE ROOM
8 BATTERY SPACE
9 CONTROL ROOM
10 CREW ACCOMMODATION

14 BEAM TORPEDO TUBES
15 FORWARD TORPEDO TUBES
16 FORWARD TORPEDO STOWAGE
22 BOILER ROOM
25 SEARCH PERISCOPE
26 ATTACK PERISCOPE
27 W/T MAST

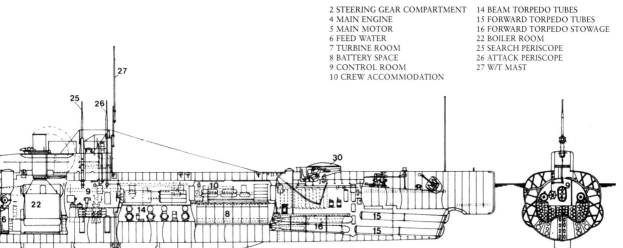

	launched	builder
K1, K2	1916	HM Dockyard, Portsmouth
K3, K4	1916	Vickers
K5	1916	HM Dockyard, Portsmouth
K6,K7	1916	HM Dockyard, Devonport
K8–K10	1916	Vickers
K11	1916	Armstrong
K12	1917	Armstrong
K13 (later K22)	1916	Fairfield
K14	1917	Fairfield
K15	1917	Scotts
K16	1917	Beardmore
K17	1917	Vickers

Specification

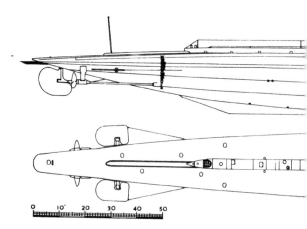

Displacement	surfaced:	1,883 tons
	submerged:	2,600 tons
Dimensions:		338 x 26½ x 16 ft
Complement:		55
Propulsion	surfaced:	Two steam geared turbines 10,000 hp, diesel engine 800 hp (auxiliary)
	submerged:	Two electric motors 1,400 hp Fuel capacity 170 tons
Speed:	surfaced:	24 knots
	submerged:	9½ knots
Armament	Gun:	Two 4 in single; one 3 in single AA; one Lewis gun (see armament note)
	Torpedo:	Eight 18 in tubes; four bow, four beam. A depth charge thrower was mounted on some boats in the Class

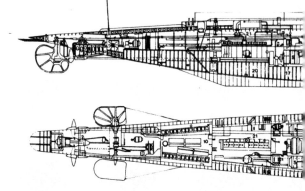

Class note: As mentioned under Swordfish Class, this design was intended to operate with the battle fleet; thus the reasons for the high surface speed and medium gun armament. After trials the height of the bow was raised to avoid a tendency in the earlier boats to trim by the bows. The change gave the extra buoyancy required, but also necessitated increasing the height of the conning tower.

Armament note: The Class was designed to be mounted with two 5.5 in guns on single mountings, but these were not fitted. It was also planned that the boats should have two 18 in torpedo tubes on a twin mounting on the upper casing for use in night attacks, but this was removed from all the boats.

1 TRIMMING TANK	15 FORWARD TORPEDO TUBES
2 STEERING GEAR COMPARTMENT	16 FORWARD TORPEDO STOWAGE
4 MAIN ENGINE	17 FUEL TANKS
5 MAIN MOTOR	19 RADIO ROOM
6 FEED WATER	20 MAIN BALLAST TANK
7 TURBINE ROOM	21 DIESEL ROOM
8 BATTERY SPACE	22 BOILER ROOM
9 CONTROL ROOM	25 SEARCH PERISCOPE
10 CREW ACCOMMODATION	26 ATTACK PERISCOPE
11 WARD ROOM	27 W/T MAST
14 BEAM TORPEDO TUBES	29 4 in GUN
	30 3 in GUN

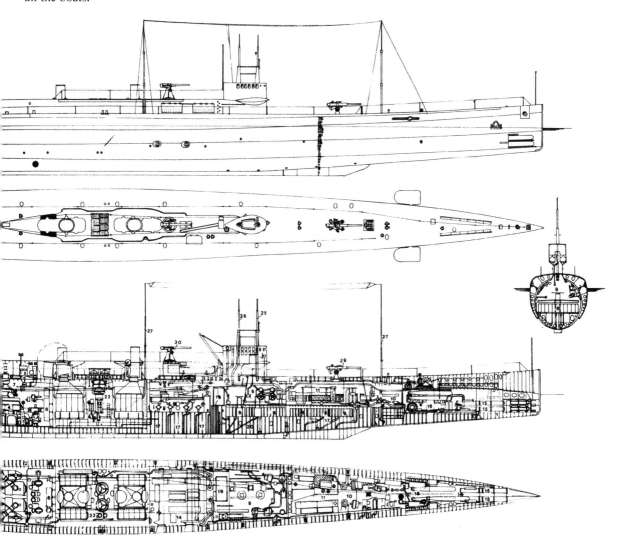

47

Losses

K1 collided with *K4* off the Danish coast on 18 November 1917. *K1* was badly damaged and her crew were taken off before she was sunk by gunfire from HMS *Blonde*.

K4 sank in collision with HMS *Inflexible* in a night exercise off May Island on 31 January 1918. The submarine, which was on the surface, altered course under the bows of the battleship.

K5 foundered in the Bay of Biscay on 20 January 1921.

K13 foundered in the Gare Loch while on builders trials on 29 January 1917. She was salvaged and renamed *K22* in March 1917.

K15 sank in Portsmouth harbour on 25 June 1921.

K17 was lost in the same night exercise as *K4* on 31 January 1918. She was rammed, after altering course, by HMS *Fearless* off May Island.

K6, showing the modified bow, open upper bridge above the conning tower, and the heightened funnels.

	launched	builder
K26	1919	Vickers (completed at HM Dockyard, Chatham)

Completion: Sept 1923

Cancellations: Five further boats on order were cancelled in Nov 1918. They were: K23–K25 (Armstrong); K27 and K28 (Vickers)

Specification

Displacement	surfaced:	2,140 tons
	submerged:	2,770 tons
Dimensions:		351¼ x 28 x 16½ ft
Complement:		58
Propulsion	surfaced:	Two steam geared turbines 10,000 hp
	submerged:	Two electric motors 1,400 hp
Speed:	surfaced:	23½ knots
	submerged:	9 knots
Armament	Gun:	Three 4 in single (see armament note)
	Torpedo:	Six 21 in bow tubes; four 18 in beam tubes

Class notes: K26 was planned to be the first of a 'follow up' to the earlier K Class. The hull was longer and she carried greater armament, but her machinery was the same. This had the understandable result that she was slower.

Armament note: The 4 in guns had 20 deg elevation and a range of 9,000 yds.

K26 during trials after World War I.

Close up view of the conning tower of K26.

L71 preparing to enter harbour. She is a group 3 boat
with 4 in guns fore and aft of the conning tower.

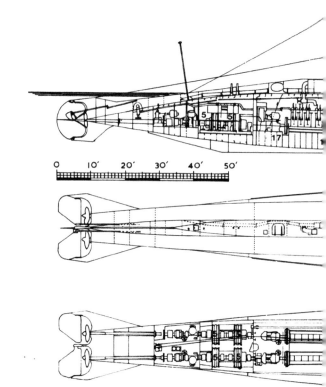

	launched	builder
Group 1		
L1 (ex E56),	1917	Vickers
L2 (ex E57),	1917	Vickers
L3, L4	1917	Vickers
L5	1918	Swan Hunter
L6	1918	Beardmore
L7, L8	1917	Cammell Laird

Specification

Displacement	surfaced:	890 tons
	submerged:	1,070 tons
Dimensions:		231 x 23½ x 14 ft
Propulsion	surfaced:	Two diesel engines 2,400 hp
	submerged:	Two electric motors 1,600 hp
		Fuel capacity 76 tons
Speed	surfaced:	17½ knots
	submerged:	10½ knots
Range	surfaced:	2,800 nm at 10 knots
Armament	Gun:	Single 3 or 4 in
	Torpedo:	Six 18 in; four bow, two beam

	launched	builder

Group 2

L9, L10	1918	Denny
L11, L12, L14	1918	Vickers
L15, L16	1918	Fairfield
L18, L19, L20	1918	Vickers
L21–L27	1919	Vickers
L33	1919	Swan Hunter
Cancellations:	L13, L36–L49 were not ordered. The following were cancelled in April 1919: L28–L31 (Vickers); L34 and L35 (HM Dockyard, Pembroke). L32 had been launched by Vickers, but was broken up	
Completion:	L23 was completed at HM Dockyard, Chatham; L26 at HM Dockyard, Portsmouth. L11, L12, L14, L17 and L25 were completed as minelayers	

Specification as Group 1 except

Displacement surfaced: 895 tons
                    submerged: 1,075 tons
Dimensions: 238½ x 23½ x 14 ft
Armament (except Minelayers)
        Gun: Single 4 in
        Torpedo: Two 21 in bow tubes;
                    two 18 in beam tubes
Armament (Minelayers)
        Gun: Single 4 in
        Torpedo: Four 21 in bow tubes
        Mines: 14

 3 MAIN ENGINE ROOM
 4 MAIN ENGINE
 5 MAIN MOTOR
 8 BATTERY SPACE
 9 CONTROL ROOM
10 CREW ACCOMMODATION
11 WARD ROOM
15 FORWARD TORPEDO TUBES
16 FORWARD TORPEDO STOWAGE
17 FUEL TANKS
25 SEARCH PERISCOPE
26 ATTACK PERISCOPE
27 W/T MAST
29 4 in GUN

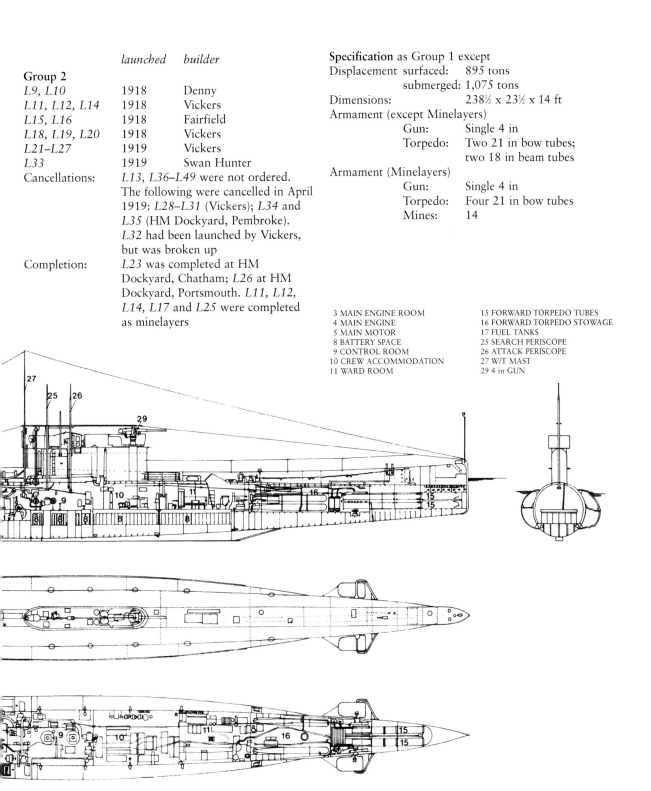

L12 with her superimposed 4 in gun. the pronounced bulk of her saddle tank shows clearly. Alongside H28 is an R Class attack submarine.

	launched	builder
Group 3		
L52	1918	Armstrong
L53	1919	Armstrong
L54	1919	Denny
L55	1918	Fairfield
L56	1919	Fairfield
L69	1918	Beardmore
L71	1919	Scotts

Cancellations: The following were cancelled: *L50*, *L51*, *L60*, *L61* (Cammell Laird); *L57*, *L58*, *L62* (Fairfield); *L59*, *L70* (Beardmore); *L63*, *L64*, *L72* (Scotts); *L65*, *L66* (Swan Hunter); *L67*, *L68* (Armstrong); *L73*, *L74* (Denny)

Completion: *L53* was completed at HM Dockyard, Chatham, *L54* at HM Dockyard, Devonport; *L69* at HM Dockyard, Rosyth. *L67* and *L68* were completed in 1927 for the Yugoslav government. They were named *Hrabri* and *Nebojsa*

Specification

Displacement	surfaced:	960 tons
	submerged:	1,150 tons
Dimensions:		235 x 23½ x 13 ft
Complement:		40
Propulsion	surfaced:	Two diesel engines 1,920 hp
	submerged:	Two electric motors 1,150 hp
		Fuel capacity 76 tons
Speed	surfaced:	17 knots
	submerged:	10½ knots

L20 leaving harbour, the casing crew stowing the mooring ropes. The anchor can be seen in its housing near the bow. The gun is slightly elevated.

Range	surfaced:	2,800 nm at 10 knots
Armament	Gun:	Two 4 in single
	Torpedo:	Six 21 in bow tubes

Class note: In the 1919 edition of *Jane's Fighting Ships* the comment is made that 'the L Class is in a highly complex state owing to the variations in build giving ten or more types by appearance'.

Armament note: *L1–L8* were designed to have two 3 in DP/HA guns, but were only fitted with one. *L11* had no deck gun. *L3*, *L12*, *L14*, *L17* and *L18* had one 4 in gun.

Losses

L9 foundered in Hong Kong harbour during a typhoon on 18 August 1923. She was salvaged.

L10 was sunk on 30 October 1918 by the German Destroyer S33 off the R. Texel.

L24 was in collision with HMS *Resolution* and sank off Portland on 10 January 1924.

L55 was forced into a minefield by the Bolshevik Destroyers *Gavril* and *Azard* in the Baltic Sea on 4 June 1919, and was sunk by gunfire. She was salvaged and recommissioned into the Soviet Navy in 1928 under her original number.

	launched	builder
M1 (ex K18)	1917	Vickers
M2 (ex K19)	1918	Vickers
M3 (ex K20)	1918	Armstrong Whitworth
Cancellation:		M4 was not completed, but sold back to Armstrong Whitworth for scrap

Specification

Displacement	surfaced:	1,600 tons
	submerged:	1,950 tons
Dimensions:		296 x 24½ x 16 ft
Complement:		60–70
Propulsion	surfaced:	Two diesel engines 2,400 hp
	submerged:	Two electric motors 1,600 hp
Speed	surfaced:	15½ knots
	submerged:	9½ knots
Range	surfaced:	3,800 nm at 10 knots
Armament	Gun:	Single 12 in; single 3 in AA (see armament note)
	Torpedo:	M1, M2: Four 18 in bow tubes. M3: Four 21 in bow tubes

Class note: These boats were a development of the K Class design and have been described as submarine monitors.

Armament note: The 12 in gun had a sufficient elevation for the muzzle (on which was a foresight; the periscope acted as the backsight) to break surface with the hull awash. In this trim the weapon could be fired, but the boat had to surface for reloading.

In M2 the 12 in gun was removed and an aircraft hangar built in its place in front of the conning tower. A gantry was fitted to lift a small sea plane with folding wings. M2 sank, reportedly due to leakage of water through the hangar door, shortly after the end of the war.

M3 was converted to a minelayer with capacity for 100 mines. The 12 in gun was removed and replaced by four machine guns. Her torpedo armament was unchanged.

M1 leaving for sea trials with some dockyard staff on board. The 12 in gun is elevated to 30°.

Losses

M1 sank after collision with SS *Vidar* off Start Point on 12 November 1926.

M2 sank as described above.

There were no war losses.

2 STEERING GEAR COMPARTMENT	11 WARD ROOM
3 MAIN ENGINE ROOM	15 FORWARD TORPEDO TUBES
4 MAIN ENGINE	16 FORWARD TORPEDO STOWAGE
5 MAIN MOTOR	17 FUEL TANKS
8 BATTERY SPACE	19 RADIO ROOM
9 CONTROL ROOM	27 W/T MAST
10 CREW ACCOMMODATION	30 3 in GUN

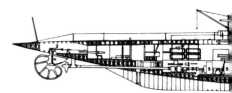

M3 converted for minelaying

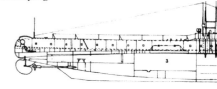

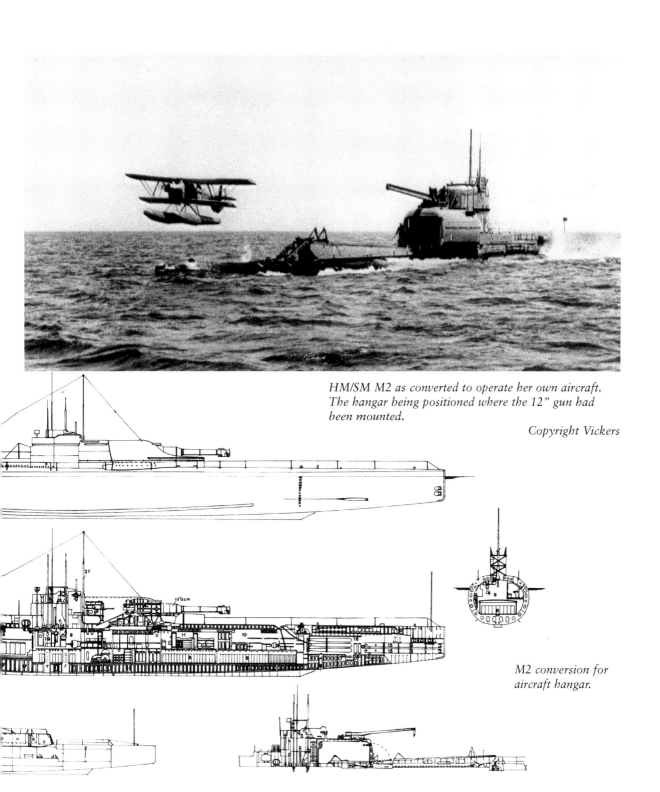

HM/SM M2 *as converted to operate her own aircraft.*
The hangar being positioned where the 12" gun had
been mounted.

Copyright Vickers

M2 *conversion for*
aircraft hangar.

	launched	builder
R1–R4	1918	HM Dockyard, Chatham
R7, R8	1918	Vickers
R9, R10	1918	Armstrong Whitworth
R11, R12	1918	Cammell Laird

Specification

Displacement	surfaced:	410 tons
	submerged:	500 tons
Dimensions:		163 x 15¾ x 11½ ft
Complement:		22
Propulsion	surfaced:	One diesel engine 240 hp
	submerged:	One electric motor 1,200 hp
Speed	surfaced:	9½ knots
	submerged:	15 knots
Range	surfaced:	2,000 nm at 8 knots
Armament	Torpedo:	Six 18 in bow tubes

R10 at anchor.

Class note: This was a splendid design of what would now be called a 'hunter-killer' submarine being designed to attack enemy U-Boats. But boats of this class were not completed until very late in the war and only one actually made an attack firing the full six-torpedo salvo at an enemy submarine (and missing).

The design was somewhat of a reversion to earlier practice by having internal ballast tanks and a streamlined hull. Consequently the gun was not fitted and the narrow stern allowed of only a single propeller shaft.

None of these boats was in service after 1925, all having been sold for scrap.

3 MAIN ENGINE ROOM	15 FORWARD TORPEDO TUBES
4 MAIN ENGINE	16 FORWARD TORPEDO STOWAGE
5 MAIN MOTOR	17 FUEL TANKS
8 BATTERY SPACE	20 MAIN BALLAST TANK
9 CONTROL ROOM	25 SEARCH PERISCOPE
10 CREW ACCOMMODATION	26 ATTACK PERISCOPE
11 WARD ROOM	27 W/T MAST

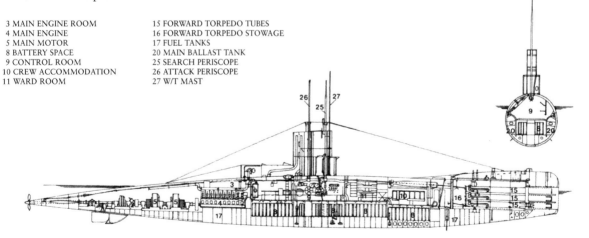

U-86 looking fully seaworthy and very modern for her time.

	completed	builder
U-86	1916	Krupp-Germania, Kiel

Specification

Displacement	surfaced:	808 tons
	submerged:	946 tons
Dimensions:		230 x 20½ ft*
Complement:		32–39
Propulsion	surfaced:	Two diesel engines 2,400 hp
	submerged:	Two electric motors 1,200 hp
Speed	surfaced:	16¾ knots
	submerged:	9 knots
Armament	Gun:	One 4.1 in; one 3.4 in
	Torpedo:	Four 19.7 in tubes; two bow, two stern

*Draught not known.

U-126 entering harbour. She is flying her number beneath the White Ensign.

	completed	builder
U-126	1918	Blohm and Voss, Hamburg

Specification

Displacement	surfaced:	1,164 tons
	submerged:	1,468 tons
Dimensions:		269 x 24½ ft*
Complement:		40
Propulsion	surfaced:	Two diesel engines 2,400 hp
	submerged:	Two electric motors 1,240 hp
Speed	surfaced:	14¾ knots
	submerged:	7¼ knots
Armament	Gun:	One or two 5.9 in
	Torpedo:	Four 19.7 in bow tubes
	Mines:	42–48 mines from two stern tubes

Note: These two submarines were commissioned into the Royal Navy under their German numbers for trials and comparisons. *U-86* was in commission from September 1919 to February 1920; *U-126* from March 1920 to September 1921. *U-86* sank in heavy weather while under tow to the breaker's yard in 1921. *U-126* was sold for breaking up in 1923.

	launched	builder
X1	1923	HM Dockyard, Chatham

X1 leaving harbour. The size of the two twin gun mountings can be appreciated in comparison with the height of the men on the casing.

Specification

Displacement	surfaced:	2,780 tons
	submerged:	3,600 tons
Dimensions:		350 bp x 29¾ x 15¾ ft
Complement:		110
Propulsion	surfaced:	Diesel engines 6,000 hp
	submerged:	Electric motors 2,600 hp
Armament	Gun:	Four 5.2 in two twin mountings with cupola-type shields; two twin mg (AA)
	Torpedo:	Six 21 in bow tubes
Speed	surfaced:	19½ knots
	submerged:	9 knots
Range	surfaced:	12,500 nm at 12 knots

Note: This design evolved from intelligence gained from the World War I Cruiser submarines of the German Navy. *X1* was produced very largely as an experiment and the gun armament was at the limit permitted in the Naval Defence Act. The boat suffered from numerous malfunctions in service; after five years she was laid up, and was scrapped in 1936. The bow of *X1* retained the shape or profile similar to the K Class boats of World War I.

Group 1

	launched	builder
O1 (later Oberon)	1926	HM Dockyard, Chatham
OA2 (later Otway)	1926	Vickers Armstrong
OA1 (later Oxley)		

Specification

Displacement	surfaced:	1,350 tons (O1 1,311 tons)
	submerged:	1,870 tons (O1 1,831 tons)
Dimensions:		275 bp x 27¾ x 13¼ ft
		(O1 270 bp x 28 x 13¼ ft)
Complement:		54
Propulsion	surfaced:	Diesel engines 3,000 bhp
	submerged:	Electric motors 1,350 bhp
		Two shafts
Speed	surfaced:	O1 17½ knots
	submerged:	OA1, OA2 15½ knots
Range	surfaced:	8,500 nm at 10 knots
Armament	Gun:	Single 4 in; two mg (AA)
	Torpedo:	Eight 21 in tubes; six bow, two stern

Osiris entering Portsmouth harbour. The radio aerials were high, as can be seen by the angle of the insulators. This Class had quite high freeboard when trimmed for surface running.

	launched	builder

Group 2

	launched	builder
Odin	1928	HM Dockyard, Chatham
Olympus	1928	Beardmore
Orpheus	1929	Beardmore
Osiris, Oswald, Otus	1928	Vickers Armstrong, Barrow-in-Furness

Specification

Displacement	surfaced:	1,475 tons
	submerged:	2,030 tons
Dimensions:		260 bp x 29¾ x 13¾ ft
Complement:		53
Propulsion	surfaced:	Diesel engines 4,400 hp
	submerged:	Electric motors 1,325 hp
		Two shafts
		Fuel capacity 200 tons

Speed and Range as Group 1
Armament as Group 1

Class note: This Class was the leading design of post-World War I submarines for the Royal Navy. There were many teething troubles, and new features were introduced. Strengthened pressure hulls were used and fuel was carried in the ballast tanks which aided rapid diving but tanks were of light construction and fuel leakage was experienced. The boats had an extended surface range. Forty-four ft periscopes were fitted and Asdic equipment.

With the exception of Nautilus and Swordfish (*c.* 1915-16) this Class were the first boats to be named.

OA2 and *OA1* were built for the Royal Australian Navy but were transferred to the Royal Navy in 1931.

Armament note: *Oberon*, designed in 1924, was intended to have either a 4 in or a 4.7 in gun with Lewis guns for AA protection.

Losses

Oxley was mistaken for a U-Boat and rammed by HM S/M *Triton* on 10 September 1939 off the coast of Norway. This was the first British naval loss in World War II.

Odin was sunk by gunfire from the Italian destroyer *Strale* in the Gulf of Taranto on 14 June 1940.

Olympus was mined and sank off Malta on 8 May 1942.

Orpheus was depth-charged by the Italian destroyer *Turbine* in the eastern Mediterranean on 27 June 1940.

Oswald was rammed by the Italian destroyer *Vivaldi* south of Calabria on 1 August 1940.

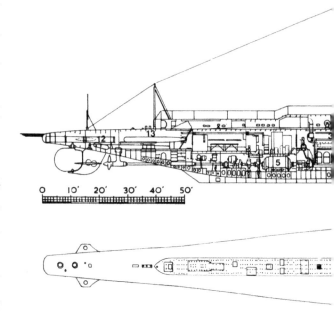

An Odin Class boat at sea.

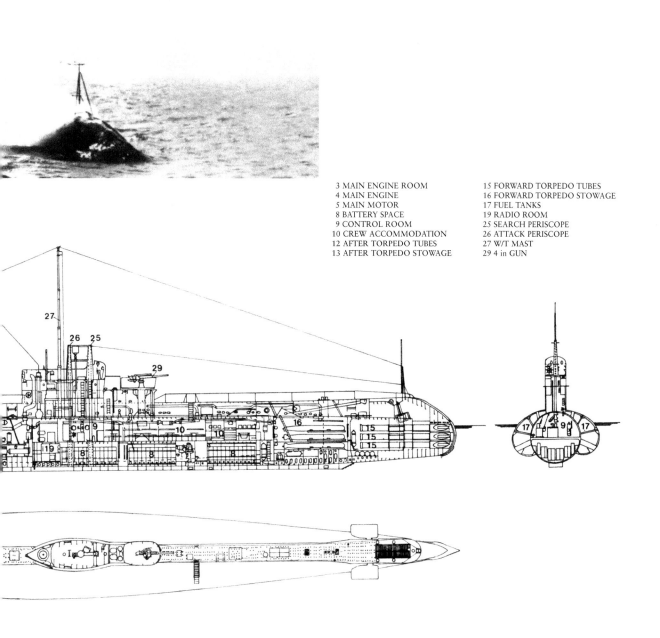

3 MAIN ENGINE ROOM
4 MAIN ENGINE
5 MAIN MOTOR
8 BATTERY SPACE
9 CONTROL ROOM
10 CREW ACCOMMODATION
12 AFTER TORPEDO TUBES
13 AFTER TORPEDO STOWAGE

15 FORWARD TORPEDO TUBES
16 FORWARD TORPEDO STOWAGE
17 FUEL TANKS
19 RADIO ROOM
25 SEARCH PERISCOPE
26 ATTACK PERISCOPE
27 W/T MAST
29 4 in GUN

Proteus exercising at sea with her 4 in gun elevated and trained to starboard.

	launched	builder
Parthion	1929	HM Dockyard, Chatham
Perseus	1929	Vickers Armstrong
Phoenix	1929	Cammell Laird
Poseidon	1929	Vickers Armstrong
Proteus	1929	Vickers Armstrong
Pandora	1929	Vickers Armstrong
(ex *Python*)		

Specification

Displacement	surfaced:	1,760 tons
	submerged:	2,040 tons
Dimensions:		289 x 28 x 13½ ft
Complement:		56
Propulsion	surfaced:	Two diesel engines 4,400 hp
	submerged:	Two electric motors 1,350 hp
		Two shafts
Armament	Gun:	One 4 in
	Torpedo:	Eight 21 in tubes, six bow and two stern
Speed	surfaced:	18 knots
	submerged:	9 knots
Range	surfaced:	8,500 nm at 10 knots

Class note: These boats had a higher surface speed than the previous O Class.

Gun armament note: *Perseus* had one 4.7 in gun on commissioning, and had this replaced temporarily with an experimental 4.9 in gun.

Losses

Parthion struck a mine and sank on 11 August 1943 in the southern Adriatic.

Perseus whilst off Zante, was sighted on 1 December 1941 and torpedoed by the Italian submarine *Enrico Toti*.

Phoenix was a contact of the Italian TB *Albatross* and was depth charged and lost off Sicily on 17 July 1940.

Pandora was bombed and sank by Italian aircraft in Valetta Dockyard on 1 April 1942.

Poseidon sank in collision with SS *Yuta* off Wei-Hai-Wei in the Gulf of Korea on 9 June 1931.

Pandora with the forward hydroplanes folded flush with the hull and the torpedo davit apparently ready for use.

	launched	builder
Rainbow	1930	HM Dockyard, Chatham
Regent, Regulus, Rover	1930	Vickers Armstrong
Cancellations:		Royalist (Beardmore) and Rupert (Cammell Laird) were cancelled in 1929.

Specification

Displacement	surfaced:	1,740 tons
	submerged:	2,015 tons
Dimensions:		287 x 28 x 13½ ft
Complement:		51
Propulsion	surfaced:	Two diesel engines 4,400 hp
	submerged:	Two electric motors 1,320 hp
Armament	Gun:	Single 4 in (see armament note)
	Torpedo:	Eight 21 in tubes; six bow, two stern
Speed	surfaced:	17½ knots
	submerged:	9 knots

Rover at speed with a crowded conning tower. This is an early design of the 'conventional' submarine.

Class note: This was the first Class to include a bathroom for those lodged in the Ward Room, but the fresh water capacity was not increased.

Armament note: As designed a 4.7 in gun was mounted, but later replaced by a 4 in gun.

Losses

Rainbow was torpedoed by the Italian submarine *Enrico Toti* off Calabria on or about 19 October 1940.

Regent was mined in the Strait of Otranto on 16 April 1943.

Regulus was lost, cause unknown, in the Strait of Otranto on 6 December 1940.

Severn on builder's trials.

	launched	builder
Thames	1932	Vickers Armstrong
Clyde, Severn	1934	Vickers Armstrong

Specification

Displacement	surfaced:	2,165 tons
	submerged:	2,680 tons
Dimensions:		325 x 28 x 13½ ft
Complement:		61
Propulsion	surfaced:	Two diesel engines 10,000 hp
	submerged:	Two electric motors 2,500 hp
Speed	surfaced:	22½ knots
	submerged:	10 knots
Range	surfaced:	12,000 nm at 8 knots
Armament	Gun:	Single 4 in
	Torpedo:	Six 21 in bow tubes

Class note: Yet again an attempt to return, albeit with conventional propulsion methods, to the Fleet Submarine similar to the K class of World War I. These boats were quite large and, it is understood, very comfortable. They were designed with a somewhat light armament for their tonnage.

Armament note: *Thames* was first fitted with one 4.7 in gun which was later replaced with a 4 in gun.

Loss

Thames was mined and sank off Norway on 23 July 1940.

	launched	builder
Group 1		
Sturgeon, Seahorse	1932	HM Dockyard, Chatham
Swordfish	1931	HM Dockyard, Chatham
Starfish	1933	HM Dockyard, Chatham

Specification

Displacement	surfaced:	735 tons
	submerged:	935 tons
Dimensions:		202½ x 24 x 12 ft
Complement:		36
Propulsion	surfaced:	Two 8 cyl diesel engines
		1,550 hp
	submerged:	Two electric motors 1,300 hp
		Fuel capacity 40 tons
Speed	surfaced:	14 knots
	submerged:	10 knots
Range	surfaced:	3,750 nm at 10 knots
Armament	Gun:	Single 3 in
	Torpedo:	Six 21 in bow tubes

	launched	builder
Group 2		
Sealion, Salmon	1934	Cammell Laird
Shark, Snapper	1934	HM Dockyard, Chatham
Seawolf	1935	Scotts
Spearfish	1936	Cammell Laird
Sunfish	1936	HM Dockyard, Chatham
Sterlet	1937	HM Dockyard, Chatham

Specification as Group 1 except:

Displacement	surfaced:	765 tons
	submerged:	960 tons
Dimensions:		length increased to 208 ft
Diving depth:		rivetted hull boats 300 ft
		welded hull boats 350 ft

	launched	builder
Group 3		
P61	1941	Cammell Laird
(later *P211, Safari*)		
P62	1942	Cammell Laird
(later *P212, Sahib*)		
P63	1942	Cammell Laird
(later *P213, Saracen*)		

Sickle after leaving the builder's yard on the Mersey. The direction finding aerial is mounted on the casing behind the 'bandstand' aft of the conning tower.

	launched	builder
P64	1942	Scotts
(later P214, Satyr)		
P65	1943	Scotts
(later P215, Sceptre)		
P66	1942	Scotts
(later P216, Seadog)		
P67	1942	Cammell Laird
(later P217, Sibyl)		
P68	1943	Scotts (completed by
(later P218, Sea Rover)		Vickers Armstrong)
P69	1941	Vickers Armstrong
(later P219, Seraph)		
P71	1941	Vickers Armstrong
(later P221, Shakespeare)		
P223	1942	Vickers Armstrong
(later Sea Nymph)		
P224 (later Sickle)	1942	Vickers Armstrong
P225 (later Simoom)	1942	Cammell Laird
P226 (later Sirdar)	1943	Scotts (completed by
		Vickers Armstrong)
P227 (later Spiteful)	1943	Scotts
P228 (later Splendid)	1942	HM Dockyard, Chatham

	launched	builder
P229	1942	HM Dockyard, Chatham
(later Sportsman)		
P231 (later Stoic)	1943	HM Dockyard, Chatham
P232	1943	HM Dockyard, Chatham
(later Stonehenge)		
P233 (later Storm)	1943	HM Dockyard, Chatham
P234	1943	Cammell Laird
(later Stratagem)		
P235	1943	Cammell Laird
(later Strongbow)		
P236 (later Spark)	1943	Scotts
P237 (later Scythian)	1944	Scotts
P238	1942	Scotts
(later Stubborn)		
P239 (later Surf)	1942	Cammell Laird
Syrtis, Spirit, Statesman,		Cammell Laird
Sturdy, Stygian,		
Shalimar	1943	HM Dockyard, Chatham
Scotsman	1944	Scotts

	launched	builder
Sea Devil	1945	Scotts
Subtle, Supreme, Sea Scout, Selene, Scorcher, Sidon, Sleuth, Solent	1944	Cammell Laird
Spearhead, Spur	1944	Cammell Laird
Seneschal, Sentinel	1945	Scotts
Saga, Springer, Sanguine	1945	Cammell Laird
Cancellations:	The following, under construction with Cammell Laird, were cancelled or broken up: *Sea Robin, Spritely, Surface* and *Surge*. The number *P230* was not allocated.	

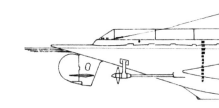

GROUP 1

Specification similar to Group 1, and diving capability as Group 2, except:

Displacement	surfaced:	814 tons
	submerged:	990 tons
Dimensions:		217 x 24 x 13¼ ft
Armament	Gun:	Some boats mounted a 4 in in lieu of the 3 in gun
	Torpedo:	Seven 21 in tubes; six bow, one stern

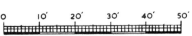

GROUP 2

(Losses are on page 70.)

Class note: This Class totalled 62 boats commissioned. The design was influenced by the Admiralty decision to standardise on a short-range and a long-range Class: this was the short-range Class and T Class (see p.74) was to fulfil the long-range role.

Group 1 were all completed by the end of 1933; mines could be carried in lieu of torpedoes. The first boat in Group 3 was numbered *P211*. Later the Prime Minister, Winston Churchill, decided that all submarines would be named. However, names were not allocated immediately to *P226* and *P230*; Sirdar was the first to be launched under her name rather than number.

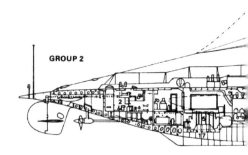

GROUP 3

Armament note: In Group 1 *Sturgeon* and *Swordfish* had a 3 in DP/HA disappearing gun; later boats in this group had a 3 in fixed gun. The boats in Group 3 carrying a 4 in gun required an increase in complement of three.

2 STEERING GEAR COMPARTMENT
3 MAIN ENGINE ROOM
4 MAIN ENGINE
5 MAIN MOTOR
8 BATTERY SPACE
9 CONTROL ROOM
10 CREW ACCOMMODATION
11 WARD ROOM
12 AFTER TORPEDO TUBES
15 FORWARD TORPEDO TUBES

16 FORWARD TORPEDO STOWAGE
17 FUEL TANKS
19 RADIO ROOM
23 'Q' TANK
25 SEARCH PERISCOPE
26 ATTACK PERISCOPE
27 W/T MAST
28 RADAR MAST
30 3 in GUN

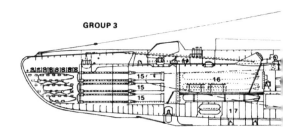

GROUP 3 MODIFIED, 1953

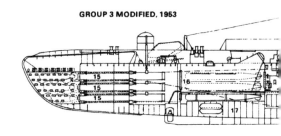

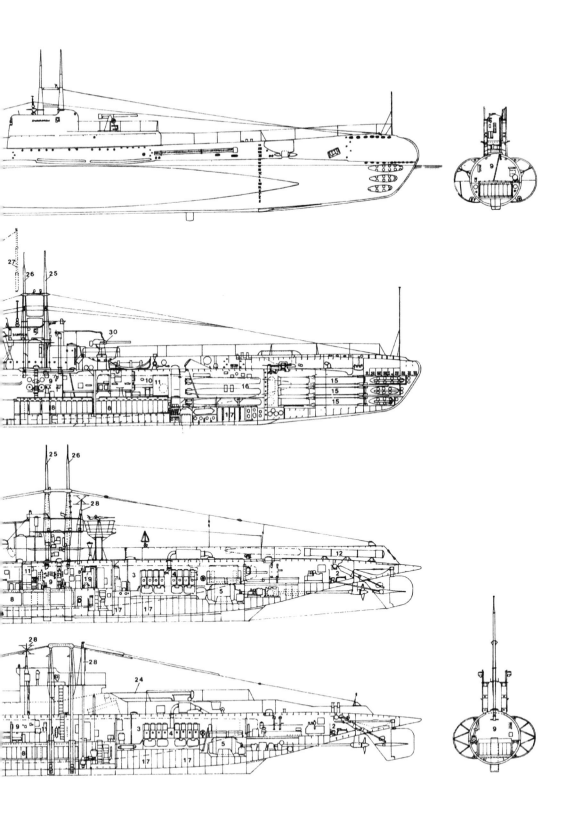

Losses

Sahib was depth-charged by the Italian escort vessel *Gabbiano* on 24 April 1943, and was abandoned and scuttled off the north coast of Sicily.

Salmon was mined in Norwegian waters on 9 July 1940.

Saracen was depth-charged and sunk by the Italian corvette *Minerva* off Bastia on 18 August 1943.

Seahorse was sunk by the German First Minesweeping flotilla in the Heligoland Bight on 7 January 1940.

Shark was sunk by German minesweepers *M1803*, *M1806* and *M1807* off Skudesneshavn, Norway, on 6 July 1940.

Sickle is believed to have been mined in the Antikitheria Channel in the eastern Mediterranean on or about 18 June 1944.

Simoom was assumed lost, cause unknown, in the Dardanelles on 19 November 1943.

Snapper was assumed lost in the Bay of Biscay, cause unknown, on 12 February 1942.

Spearfish was torpedoed by *U-34* off the coast of Norway sometime before 5 August 1940.

Splendid was sunk by the German destroyer *Hermes** off the west coast of Corsica on 21 April 1943.†

Starfish was depth charged and sunk by the German minesweeper *M7* in the Heligoland Bight on 9 January 1940.

Sterlet was depth charged by the German anti-submarine trawlers *UJ125*, *UJ126* and *UJ127* in the Skaggerak on 18 April 1940.

Stonehenge was lost, cause unknown, off the Nicobar Islands on or about 22 March 1944.

Stratagem was depth charged and sunk by a Japanese patrol craft off Malacca on 22 November 1943.

Swordfish was lost, cause unknown, off Ushant on or about 16 November 1940.

Syrtis was mined off Bodo, Norway, on 28 March 1944.

P222 was sunk by the Italian TB *Fortunale* off Naples on 12 December 1942.

Sportsman sank off Toulon on 24 September 1952 while on loan to the French Navy.

Sidon was wrecked by an accidental torpedo explosion in Portland dockyard on 16 May 1955.

Sunfish was sunk in error by Allied aircraft on 27 July 1944. She was on passage to Murmansk for transfer to the Russian Navy as *B1*.

†The Greek Destroyer *Vasilevs Georgios* had been built in the UK as an export order by Cammell Laird but was captured by the German Navy. She looked very much like

Simoom in an almost identical situation to Sickle. Simmom has the high HF/DF aerial on the conning tower in addition to the DF type on the after casing.

a Destroyer of the Royal Navy and a number of our S/M Captains took her to be so, hence the CO of *Splendid* did not recognise *Hermes* as an enemy vessel and so this led to her loss

**Hermes* had been taken over from the Greek Navy, in which she was named *Vasilevs Georgios*.

A bow view of HM S/M Stratagem wearing the white ensign but on a buoy.

	launched	builder
Grampus	1936	HM Dockyard, Chatham
Porpoise	1932	Vickers Armstrong, Barrow-in-Furness
Narwhal	1935	Vickers Armstrong, Barrow-in-Furness
Rorqual	1936	Vickers Armstrong, Barrow-in-Furness
Cachalot	1937	Scotts
Seal	1938	HM Dockyard, Chatham
Cancellations:		*P411, P412* and *P413,* all with Scotts, were cancelled in 1941

Specification

Displacement	surfaced:	1,520 tons (*Porpoise* 1,500 tons)
	submerged:	2,157 tons (*Porpoise* 2,055 tons)
Dimensions:		289 x 25½ x 15½ ft (*Porpoise* 288 x 30 x 14 ft)
Complement:		59
Propulsion	surfaced:	Two diesel engines 3,300 bhp
	submerged:	Two electric motors 1,630 bhp
Speed	surfaced:	15 knots
	submerged:	9 knots
Range	surfaced:	7,500 nm at 10 knots
Armament	Gun:	Single 4 in
	Torpedo:	Six 21 in bow tube
	Mines:	50

Class note: The Class was intended to succeed the M Class. The periscope standards were offset vertically to starboard within the inner conning tower to allow a clear run for the mine-carrying railway which ran down the centre line from the inner bow to the outer stern doors. Compensating ballast was carried on the port side to ensure stability.

Losses

Cachalot was rammed by an Italian TB off Cyrenaica on 4 August 1941.
Grampus was depth charged by the Italian TBs *Circe* and *Clio* off Augusta, on 24 June 1940.
Narwhal was lost, cause unknown, off the Norwegian coast on or about 1 August 1940.
Porpoise was bombed by Japanese aircraft in the Malacca Strait on 19 January 1945. She was the last Royal Navy submarine to be lost in World War II.

Narwhal on the surface at speed.

Seal was captured in the Kattegat on 5 May 1940. She was spotted by German aircraft and, the water being too shallow to allow a full dive, her Captain and crew abandoned her. They were taken prisoner and the Germans had a splendid gift, which they evaluated and commissioned as *U-4.*

2 STEERING GEAR COMPARTMENT
3 MAIN ENGINE ROOM
4 MAIN ENGINE
5 MAIN MOTOR
8 BATTERY SPACE
9 CONTROL ROOM
10 CREW ACCOMMODATION
11 WARD ROOM
15 FORWARD TORPEDO TUBES
16 FORWARD TORPEDO STOWAGE
19 RADIO ROOM
25 SEARCH PERISCOPE
26 ATTACK PERISCOPE
27 W/T MAST
29 4 in GUN

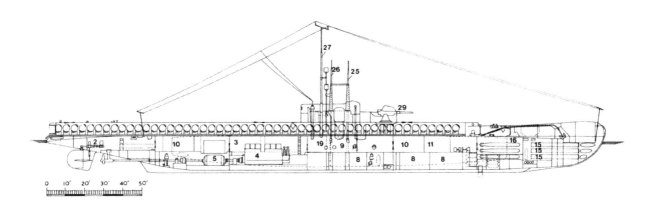

Usk on builder's trials.

Group 1

	launched	builder
Undine	1937	Vickers Armstrong, Barrow-in-Furness
Unity, Ursula	1938	Vickers Armstrong, Barrow-in-Furness
Umpire (ex P31)*	1940	HM Dockyard, Chatham
Una (ex P32)	1941	HM Dockyard, Chatham

Unbeaten (ex P33) Undaunted (ex P34) Union (ex P35)
  Unique (ex P36) Upholder (ex P37) Upright (ex P38)
  Urchin (ex P39) Urge (ex P40) Usk (ex P41)

	launched	builder
Utmost (ex P42)	1940	Vickers Armstrong, Barrow-in-Furness

*Each of the Class from *Umpire* onwards had the name changed to a number and later reverted to the original name.

Specification

Displacement	surfaced:	540 tons
	submerged:	730 tons
Dimensions:		191½ x 16 x 12¾ ft (*Umpire, Una, Unbeaten, Undaunted, Union, Urchin, Urge* and *Usk* were 196¾ ft long; beam and draft unchanged)
Complement:		31 (except *Undine, Unity* and *Ursula*: 27)
Propulsion	surfaced:	Two diesel engines 615 bhp
	submerged:	Two electric motors 825 bhp Fuel capacity 41 tons
Speed	surfaced:	11¾ knots
	submerged:	9 knots

Range	surfaced:	4,100 nm at 10 knots
Diving depth:		Group 1 and 2,200 ft
Armament	Gun:	Single 3 in or 12 pdr (except *Undine* and *Unity*)
	Torpedo:	Six 21 in bow tubes, four internal, 2 external (*Umpire, Una, Unbeaten, Undaunted, Union, Urchin, Urge* and *Usk* had four 21 in bow tubes only)

Group 2

	launched	builder
P31 (II) (ex Ullswater, later Uproar), P32	1940	Vickers Armstrong, Barrow-in-Furness

P33, P34 (II) (later *Ultimatum*), P35 (II)
(later *Umbra*), P36, P37 (II) (later *Unbending*),
P38, P39, P41 (II), P42 (II) (later *Unbroken*),
P43 (later *Unison*), P44 (later *United*), P46

	launched	builder
(later Unruffled)	1941	Vickers Armstrong, Barrow-in-Furness

P45 (later *Unrivalled*), P47, P48, P49 (later *Unruly*),
P51 (later *Unseen*), P52, P53 (later *Ultor*), P54

	launched	builder
(later Unshaken)	1942	Vickers Armstrong, Barrow-in-Furness

P55 (later *Unsparing*), P56 (later *Usurper*), P57
(later *Universal*), P58 (later *Untamed*), P59

	launched	builder
(later Untiring)	1942	Vickers Armstrong, Newcastle upon Tyne

P61 (later *Varangian*), P62 (later *Uther*), P63

	launched	builder
(later Unswerving)	1943	Vickers Armstrong, Newcastle upon Tyne

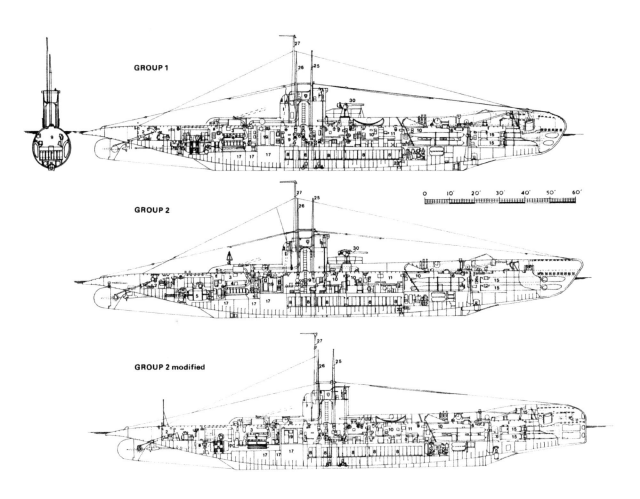

GROUP 1

GROUP 2

GROUP 2 modified

P64 (later *Vandal*), P65
(later *Upstart*)   1942   Vickers Armstrong,
                                         Barrow-in-Furness

P66 (later *Varne I*), P67
(later *Vox I*)   1943   Vickers Armstrong,
                                         Barrow-in-Furness

Specification as Group 1 except:
Displacement surfaced: 545 tons
              submerged: 740 tons
Dimensions: This Group was 197 ft long;
                             beam and draught as Group 1
Armament Gun: Single 3 in or three
                             machine guns
          Torpedo: Four 21 in bow tubes

2 STEERING GEAR COMPARTMENT
3 MAIN ENGINE ROOM
4 MAIN ENGINE
5 MAIN MOTOR
8 BATTERY SPACE
9 CONTROL ROOM
10 CREW ACCOMMODATION
11 WARD ROOM
15 FORWARD TORPEDO TUBES
16 FORWARD TORPEDO STOWAGE
17 FUEL TANKS
19 RADIO ROOM
23 'Q' TANK
25 SEARCH PERISCOPE
26 ATTACK PERISCOPE
27 W/T MAST
30 3 in GUN

Cancellations: *P81–P87, Veto, Virlie, Visitant,
                        Upas, Ulex, Utopia* (Vickers
                        Armstrong, Barrow-in-Furness);
                        *Unbridled, Upward, Vantage,
                        Vehement, Vemon, Verve* and a
                        further eight unnamed (Vickers
                        Armstrong, Newcastle upon Tyne)

Class note: The Class was initially designed for training purposes, without armament which was fitted later. They were very small but handy boats of single hull construction with internal fuel and ballast compartments.

Losses

Undine was depth charged by German minesweepers M1201, M1204 and M1207 in the Heligoland Bight on 7 January 1940.

Unity sank in a surface collision with SS Atle Jarl off the River Tyne on 29 April 1940.

Umpire was mistaken for a U-boat by the anti-submarine trawler Peter Hendriks off the Wash and rammed on 19 July 1941.

Unbeaten was mistaken for a U-boat in the Bay of Biscay and bombed by the RAF on 11 November 1942.

Undaunted was lost, cause unknown, off Tripoli on 13 May 1941.

Union was sunk by Italian patrol craft off the Tunisian coast on 22 July 1941.

Unique was lost, cause unknown, to the west of Gibraltar on 24 October 1942.

Upholder was depth charged by the Italian TB Pegaso off Tripoli on 14 April 1942.

Urge was depth charged by the Italian TB Pegaso off Tripoli on 28 April 1942.

Usk was mined and sank off Cape Bon on 3 May 1941.

Utmost was depth charged by the Italian TB Groppo off the west coast of Sicily on 24 November 1942.

P32 was mined off Tripoli on 18 August 1941.

U Class boat at sea

P33 is believed to have been mined off Tripoli on 20 August 1941.

P36 was bombed by Italian aircraft in Sliema Creek, Valetta, on 1 April 1942.

P38 was depth charged by the Italian TB Circe and Usodimare off the Tunisian coast on 26 February 1942.

P39 was bombed in Valetta harbour on 26 March 1942.

RNN Uredd (ex P41) was lost, cause unknown, in the Bodo area off the Norwegian coast on or about 24 February 1943.

P48 was depth charged by the Italian corvette Ardente in the Gulf of Tunis on 25 December 1942.

P56 was depth charged by the German patrol boat UJ-2208 in the Gulf of Genoa on 11 October 1943.

P58 was lost in an accident in the Clyde submarine exercise area on 30 May 1943. She was salvaged and recommissioned as Vitality.

Vandal foundered in the Firth of Clyde on 24 February 1943.

	launched	builder
Upshot, Variance, Vengeful, Vineyard	1944	Vickers Armstrong, Barrow-in-Furness
Urtica, Vagabond, Varne (II), Virulent, Volatile, Vortex, Votary	1944	Vickers Armstrong, Newcastle upon Tyne
Vampire, Vivid, Voracious, Vulpine	1943	Vickers Armstrong, Newcastle upon Tyne
Veldt, Venturer, Vigorous, Viking, Virtue, Visigoth, Vox (II)	1943	Vickers Armstrong, Barrow-in-Furness
Cancellations:		Ulex, Unbridled, Upas, Upward, Utopia, Vantage, Vehement, Vemon, Verve, Veto, Virile, Visitant (Vickers Armstrong at either Tyne or Barrow).

Venturer in the Clyde exercise area.

Specification

Displacement	surfaced:	545 tons
	submerged:	740 tons
Dimensions:		204½ x 16 x 12¾ ft
Complement:		37
Propulsion	surfaced:	Two diesel engines 800 bhp
	submerged:	Two electric motors 760 bhp
Speed	surfaced:	13 knots
	submerged:	9 knots
Range	surfaced:	4,050 nm at 10 knots
Diving depth:		300 ft
Armament	Gun:	Single 3 in
	Torpedo:	Four 21 in bow tubes

Class note: The U and V Classes were very largely comprised of boats of the same design (similar to the V and W Classes of destroyers in World War I) and were arbitrarily split into two named groups.

Upshot leaving Barrow. She has the DF aerial mounted on the pressure hull.

Teredo at sea. The aft-firing tubes on the casing are noticeable as are the tubes in the bow and stern casing.

	launched	builder
Group 1		
Triton	1937	Vickers Armstrong, Barrow-in-Furness
Thetis (later Thunderbolt),		
Trident	1938	Cammell Laird
Tribune	1938	Scotts
Triumph, Thistle	1938	Vickers Armstrong, Barrow-in-Furness
Taku	1939	Cammell Laird
Tarpon	1939	Scotts
Tigris	1939	HM Dockyard, Chatham
Triad, Truant, Tetrarch	1939	Vickers Armstrong, Barrow-in-Furness
Tuna	1940	Scotts
Talisman, Thrasher	1940	Cammell Laird
Torbay	1940	HM Dockyard, Chatham
Tempest, Thorn	1941	Cammell Laird
Traveller	1941	Scotts
Trusty, Turbulent	1941	Vickers Armstrong, Barrow-in-Furness
Trooper	1942	Scotts

Specification

Displacement	surfaced:	1,325 tons (*Triton* 1,095 tons)
	submerged:	1,580 tons (*Triton* 1,579 tons)
Dimensions:		274 x 26½ x 16¼ ft
Complement:		59
Propulsion	surfaced:	Two diesel engines 2,500 hp
	submerged:	Two electric motors 1,450 hp
		Two shafts
		Fuel capacity 210 tons
Speed	surfaced:	15¼ knots
	submerged:	9 knots
Range	surfaced:	9,510 nm
Diving depth:		Rivetted hull boats 300 ft
		Welded hull boats 350 ft
Armament	Gun:	Single 4 in
	Torpedo:	Ten 21 in tubes, six internal and two external at the bow; one tube on each beam (see armament note)

launched builder

Group 2

P91 (ex _Tutankhamen_, later _P311_),
Tactician (ex _P94_, later _P314_),
Taurus (ex _P93_, _P313_, later _P339_),
Templar (ex _P96_,   Vickers Armstrong,
later _P316_)   1942   Barrow-in-Furness

P325 (later _Thule_)   1942   HM Dockyard,
                                     Devonport

P327 (later _Tireless_),   HM Dockyard,
P328 (later _Token_)   1943   Portsmouth

P92 (ex _P312_, later _Trespasser_), P95 (ex _P315_,
later _Truculent_)   1942   Vickers Armstrong,
                                     Barrow-in-Furness

P326 (later _Tudor_)   1942   HM Dockyard,
                                     Devonport

P322 (later _Talent (I)_), P99 (ex _P319_,
later _Tantivy_)   1943   Vickers Armstrong,
                                     Barrow-in-Furness
                                     completed by
                                     Clydebank

P97 (ex _P317_,   Vickers Armstrong,
later _Tally-Ho_)   1942   Barrow-in-Furness
                                     completed by
                                     Clydebank

P98 (ex _P318_, later _Tantalus_), P321 (later _Telemachus_),

P324 (later _Thorough_) 1943   Vickers Armstrong,
                                     Barrow-in-Furness

P323 (later _Terrapin_) 1943   Vickers Armstrong,
                                     Barrow-in-Furness
                                     completed by Bellis &
                                     Morcom

Tiptoe, Trump, Tapir   1944   Vickers Armstrong,
                                     Barrow-in-Furness
                                     completed by
                                     Clydebank

Totem   1943   HM Dockyard,
                                     Devonport

P329 (later _Tradewind_) 1942   HM Dockyard,
                                     Chatham

Trenchant   1943   HM Dockyard,
                                     Chatham

Taciturn   1944   Vickers Armstrong,
                                     Barrow-in-Furness
                                     completed by Bellis &
                                     Morcom

Tabard   1945   Scotts

Truncheon   1944   HM Dockyard,
                                     Devonport

Turpin   1944   HM Dockyard,
                                     Chatham

Tarn   1944   Vickers Armstrong,

Tasman (later *Talent III*)	1945	Barrow-in-Furness Vickers Armstrong, Barrow-in-Furness completed by Bellis & Morcom
Teredo	1945	Vickers Armstrong, Barrow-in-Furness completed by Clydebank
Thermopylae	1945	HM Dockyard, Chatham
Cancellations:		*Talent II* (Scotts); *Theban, Threat* (Vickers Armstrong, Barrow-in-Furness); *Thor, Tiara* (HM Dockyard, Portsmouth). *Typhoon* was projected but not ordered

Specification

Displacement	surfaced:	1,090 tons
	submerged:	1,575 tons
Dimensions:		275 x 26½ x 14¾ ft
Complement:		65
Propulsion and speed		as Group 1
Range:		11,000 nm at 10 knots
Diving depth:		as Group 1
Armament	Gun:	Single 4 in, single 20 mm, three mg
	Torpedo:	Eleven 21 in tubes: six internal and two external at the bow; two mounted externally on either beam aft of the conning tower, firing aft; one external at the stern

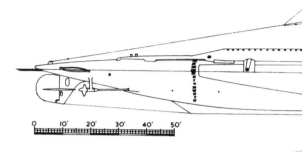

GROUP 1, 1938

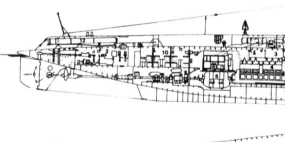

GROUP 3, 1946

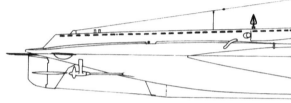

Tireless and Alaric moored at Trafford Wharf, Manchester, for the Queen's Coronation, 1953. Note the differences in their sterns.

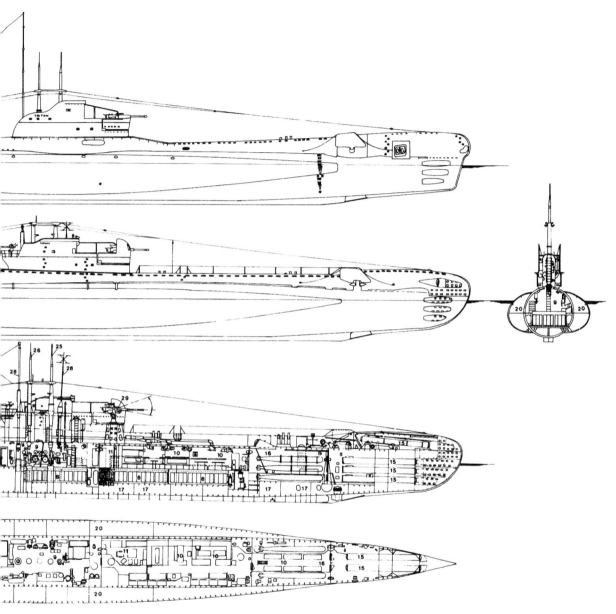

2 STEERING GEAR COMPARTMENT
3 MAIN ENGINE ROOM
4 MAIN ENGINE
5 MAIN MOTOR
8 BATTERY SPACE
9 CONTROL ROOM
10 CREW ACCOMMODATION
11 WARD ROOM
12 TORPEDO TUBES

15 FORWARD TORPEDO TUBES
16 FORWARD TORPEDO STOWAGE
17 FUEL TANKS
19 RADIO ROOM
20 MAIN BALLAST TANK
25 SEARCH PERISCOPE
26 ATTACK PERISCOPE
28 RADAR MAST
29 4 in GUN

Class note: This Class was the first to be fitted with Radar and, later, Snorkel equipment.

Armament note: This Class gave the guns a steadier firing platform for surface action. In Group 1 a salvo of ten torpedoes was available for firing forward: the two beam tubes (just aft of the conning tower) were angled outwards to clear the forward hydroplanes.

The external tubes could not be reloaded until the boat returned to harbour.

Losses

Talisman was lost, cause unknown, on or before 18 September 1942 in the Sicilian Channel.

Tarpon was sunk by the German minesweeper *M6* in the North Sea on 14 April 1940.

Triton was sunk by the Italian TB *Clio* in the Adriatic Sea on 8 December 1940.

Tempest was depth charged by the Italian TB *Circe* in the Gulf of Taranto on 13 February 1942.

Tetrarch was lost, cause unknown, in the western Mediterranean on or about 2 November 1941.

Thistle was torpedoed by *U-4* off Skudesneshavn, Norway, on 10 April 1940.

Thorn was depth charged by the Italian TB *Pegaso* off Torbruk on 6 August 1942.

Tigris was lost, cause unknown, on or about 10 March 1943 in the Gulf of Naples.

Traveller was lost, cause unknown, in the Gulf of Taranto on or about 12 December 1942.

Triad was lost, cause unknown, off the coast of Libya on or about 20 October 1940.

Triumph was lost, cause unknown, in the Aegean Sea on or about 14 January 1942.

Trooper was lost, possibly mined, in the Aegean Sea on or about 17 October 1943.

Turbulent was depth charged by an Italian MA/SB off the coast of Sardinia on or about 23 March 1943.

Thetis foundered while on trial in Liverpool Bay on 1 June 1939. After some successful dives she failed to surface and the escort vessel reported the then equivalent of 'subsunk'. Salvage vessels arrived late on the scene and *Thetis*'s stern broke surface for long enough for a hole to be cut in the hull. Only two men were rescued and the air grew foul in the submarine. Despite the salvage vessels and destroyer flotilla on the surface she could not be saved. She was salvaged and re-commissioned as *Thunderbolt*.

Thunderbolt was depth charged by the Italian MA/SB *Cicogna* north of Sicily on 13 March 1943.

The conning tower of Tally-Ho. The AA gun has been removed from the 'bandstand'.

P311 was mined and sank north of Corsica on or about 8 January 1943.

Terrapin survived a depth charge attack in the Pacific by Japanese surface craft on 19 May 1945, but was declared a constructive loss on her return to harbour.

Truculent sank after collision with the MV *Dvina* in the Medway estuary on 12 January 1950.

Tally-Ho from the air.

	launched	builder
P511 (ex R3)	1919	Fore River
P512 (ex R17)	1917	Union Iron Works
P514 (ex R19)	1918	Union Iron Works

One of the ex-US Navy R Class. Note the silhouette of the gun by comparison with the British 3 or 4 in piece.

Specification

Displacement	surfaced:	569 tons
	submerged:	680 tons
Dimensions:		179 wl x 18¼ x 14½ ft
Complement:		33
Propulsion	surfaced:	Two diesel engines 880 bhp
	submerged:	Two electric motors 934 bhp
Speed	surfaced:	13½ knots
	submerged:	10½ knots
Armament	Gun:	Single 3 in
	Torpedo:	Four 21 in bow tubes

Class note: On a similar principle to the 'Destroyers for Bases' agreement between the US and UK governments, nine submarines (this and the S Class), albeit rather ancient but none the less welcome, were transferred to the Royal Navy.

P511 and *P512*, although operational, were de-rated for training. *P511* operated from north-east Scotland; *P512* from Bermuda, on loan to the Royal Canadian Navy.

Loss

P514 was mistaken for U-boat and rammed by the Fleet minesweeper HMCS *Georgian* in the western Atlantic on 26 June 1942.

	launched	builder
P552 (ex S1)	1918	Fore River
P553 (ex S21),		
P554 (ex S22)	1920	Bethlehem Shipbuilders
P555 (ex S24), P556 (ex S29),		
P551 (ex S25)	1922	Bethlehem Shipbuilders

Specification

Displacement	surfaced:	854 tons
	submerged:	1,062 tons
Dimensions:		211 wl x 20¾ x 16 ft
Complement:		42
Propulsion	surfaced:	Two diesel engines 1,200 bhp
	submerged:	Two electric motors 1,500 bhp
		Fuel capacity 400 tons
Speed	surfaced:	14 knots
	submerged:	11 knots
Range	surfaced:	8,000 nm at 10 knots
Armament	Gun:	Single 4 in
	Torpedo:	Four 21 in bow tubes

P555 under way in harbour.

Class note: Supplied to the Royal Navy under the same terms as ex USN R Class.

Loss

P551 was mistaken for a U-boat off northern Norway and attacked by the destroyer *St Albans* and the minesweeper *Seagull* on 2 May 1942.

P614 off Rothesay.

	launched	builder
P611, P612,		Vickers Armstrong,
P614, P615	1940	Barrow-in-Furness

Specification

Displacement	surfaced:	683 tons
	submerged:	856 tons
Dimensions:		193 bp x 22¼ x 10½ ft
Complement:		41
Propulsion	surfaced:	Two diesel engines 1,550 bhp
	submerged:	Two electric motors
		1,300 bhp
		Fuel capacity 40 tons
Speed	surfaced:	13¾ knots
	submerged:	10 knots
Range	surfaced:	6,500 nm
Armament	Gun:	Single 3 in
	Torpedo:	Four 21 in tubes, four
		internal bow,
		one external stern

Class note: These four boats were under construction for the Turkish Navy at the outbreak of World War II.

P611 and *P612* were required urgently by Turkey. It was arranged that they would be fully commissioned in the Royal Navy and 'work their passage' to Turkey. They were armed, but were not to seek the enemy, as their first priority was to reach their destination safely and speedily. They were also to carry important stores and personnel to Malta en route (though this was abandoned). Their departure from the Clyde was delayed for rectification of a design fault which made them unstable at submerged speeds over six knots, but they sailed on 26 March 1942. *P611* left Gibraltar on 7 April and thereafter travelled submerged by day with a planned passage of 100 miles a day. She reached Alexandria on 25 April (having reported a possible submarine on patrol off Algiers) and the Turkish naval base at Iskanderun on 9 May. *P612* had been delayed by a steering fault at Gibraltar and followed a week later. Their crews returned to the UK. Before delivery to Turkey *P612* was used as a training boat at Portsmouth. *P614* and *P615* were also commissioned in the RN and were used for training in South Africa. Under the Turkish flag they were *P611—Oruc Reis*, *P612—Murat Reis*, *P614—Burak Reis*; *P615* would have been named *Uluc Ali Reis*.

Loss

P615 was torpedoed by *U-123* off the west African coast on 15 April 1943.

Graph (ex U-570) during evaluation in Scottish waters.

	launched	*builder*
N46 (ex *U-570*)	1941	Blohm and Voss

Specification

Displacement	surfaced:	769 tons
	submerged:	871 tons
Dimensions:		213 bp x 20¼ x 15¾ ft
Complement:		44
Propulsion	surfaced:	Two diesel engines 2,800 bhp
	submerged:	Two electric motors 750 bhp
		Two shafts
Speed	surfaced:	17 knots
	submerged:	7½ knots
Armament	Gun:	Single 3.5 in; single 37 mm (AA); Two 20 mm (AA) in twin mounting
	Torpedo:	Five 21 in tubes, four bow, one stern

Class note: This was a standard Type VIIC U-boat, captured on 28 August 1941 after an attack by Coastal Command aircraft. Having been badly damaged in the first attack and being unable to dive because of flooding, she surrendered on the second attack. While aircraft maintained watch, the Royal Navy put on a boarding party and her crew were taken prisoner. This 'gift from the gods' as the Admiralty must have regarded her, was steamed with the aid of tugs to the UK to be thoroughly evaluated. She was then repaired and, as the RN was short of submarines, commissioned as HM S/M *Graph*, the name of the operation which had been her downfall. It was a similar fate to that suffered by *Seal*—see page 72.

Loss
On 20 March 1944 she was wrecked on the west coast of the Isle of Islay.

Another view of Graph.

Perla when she was commissioned in the Italian Navy.

	launched	builder
P711 (ex *Galileo Galilei*)	1934	Tosi

Specification

Displacement	surfaced:	880 tons
	submerged:	1,231 tons
Dimensions:		231¼ bp x 22½ x 13 ft
Complement:		49
Propulsion	surfaced:	Two diesel engines 3,000 bhp
	submerged:	Two electric motors 1,300 bhp
Speed	surfaced:	17 knots
	submerged:	8½ knots
Armament	Gun:	Single 3.9 in, two 13 mm AA on single mountings
	Torpedo:	Eight 21 in tubes, four bow, four stern

	launched	builder
P712 (ex *Perla*)	1936	Adriatico

Specification

Displacement	surfaced:	620 tons
	submerged:	853 tons
Dimensions:		197 bp x 21 x 13 ft
Complement:		41
Propulsion	surfaced:	Two diesel engines 1,350 bhp
	submerged:	Two electric motors 800 bhp
Speed	surfaced:	14 knots
	submerged:	8 knots
Armament	Gun:	as *P711*
	Torpedo:	Six 21 in bow tubes

Bronzo when in commission with the Italian Navy.

	launched	builder
P714 (ex *Bronzo*)	1941	Tosi

Specification

Displacement	surfaced:	629 tons
	submerged:	864 tons
Dimensions:		197¼ bp x 21¼ x 15½ ft
Complement:		48
Propulsion		as *P712*
Speed	surfaced:	14½ knots
	submerged:	7 knots
Armament	Gun:	Single 3.9 in, four 13 mm AA on two twin mountings
	Torpedo:	Six 21 in tubes, four bow, two stern

Class note: *P711* had been attacked and disabled by the anti-submarine trawler *Moonstone* on 19 June 1940. She was taken into Aden and later to Alexandria for evaluation and was commissioned into the Royal Navy for use in training in the Mediterranean and the East Indies.

P712 was captured at Augusta, Sicily, on 9 July 1943. After evaluation she was commissioned as an operational boat and served in the Mediterranean until the end of World War II.

P714 was captured at Augusta, Sicily, on 12 July 1943. After evaluation she was commissioned as an operational boat in the Mediterranean. In 1944 she was transferred to the French Navy.

An X craft on trials.

X Prototype Class

	built	builder
X3, X4	1942	Varley Marine

Specification

Displacement	surfaced:	27 tons
	submerged:	30 tons
Dimensions:		50 x 5½ x 5½ ft
Complement:		3
Propulsion	surfaced:	Diesel engine 42 bhp
	submerged:	Electric motor 25 bhp
Speed	surfaced:	6½ knots
	submerged:	4½ knots
Range	surfaced:	1,100 nm
	submerged:	85 nm
Armament:		'Side cargoes', port and starboard; limpet mines

X Operational Class

	built	builder
X5	1942	Vickers Armstrong, Barrow-in-Furness
X6–X10	1942/45	Vickers Armstrong, Barrow-in-Furness
X20–X21	1942/45	Broadbent (Huddersfield)
X22–X23	1942/45	Markam (Chesterfield)
X24–X25	1942/45	Marshall (Gainsborough)

Specification

Displacement:		as Prototype Class
Dimensions:		51¼ bp x 5¾ x 5¾ ft
Complement:		4
Propulsion	surfaced:	Diesel engine 42 bhp
	submerged:	Electric motor 30 bhp
Speed	surfaced:	6½ knots
	submerged:	5½ knots

Range	surfaced:	1,300 nm
	submerged:	80 nm
Armament:		as Prototype Class

XE Operational Class (Pacific)

	built	builder
XE1–XE12	1944–5	Consortium of Broadbent, Markam (Chesterfield) & Marshall (Gainsborough)
XE20–XE25	1944	Vickers Armstrong, Barrow-in-Furness

Specification

Displacement	surfaced:	30 tons
	submerged:	34 tons
Dimensions:		53 x 5¾ x 5¾ ft
Propulsion:		as X5–X9
Speed	surfaced:	6½ knots
	submerged:	6 knots
Range	surfaced:	1,800 nm
	submerged:	130 nm
Armament:		as X5–X9

XT Training Class

	built	builder
XT1–XT6	1944	Vickers Armstrong, Barrow-in-Furness

Specification as XE Class
XE10 was cancelled in 1945

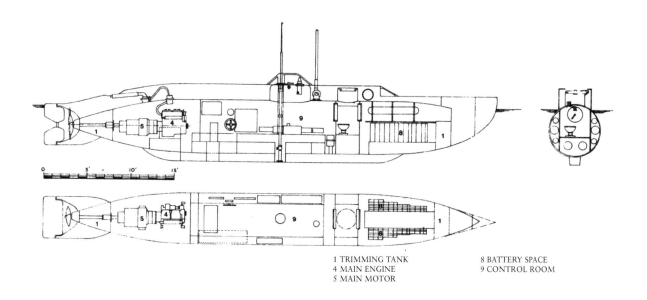

1 TRIMMING TANK   8 BATTERY SPACE
4 MAIN ENGINE   9 CONTROL ROOM
5 MAIN MOTOR

An XT craft after completion by Vickers.

X Class (post war)

	built	builder
X51–X54 (Minnow, Stickleback, Shrimp and Sprat)	1954	Vickers Armstrong, Barrow-in-Furness

Specification

Displacement	surfaced:	36 tons
	submerged:	41 tons
Dimensions:		53¾ x 6¼ x 7½ ft
Complement:		5
Propulsion	surfaced:	6 cyl diesel engine
	submerged:	Electric motors, One shaft
Speed	surfaced:	7 knots
	submerged:	6 knots
Armament:		As XE Class
Cancellation:		*X10* was cancelled when partially built

Class notes: The idea of a midget submarine may have been evolved from the successes by Italian naval personnel in disabling Royal Naval ships in Alexandria harbour in the earlier part of World War II. The first two X craft were built as prototypes by a company which had never built submarines before. They were much too small to carry torpedoes and their size was governed by the object of entering heavily guarded and secluded bases and harbours

Minnow with her free-flooding side cargoes fitted.

of the enemy. It will be noted from the dimensions that no man could stand upright in one of these craft. When being 'driven' on the surface, the commanding officer stood on the casing with a harness to secure him; and steering and other controls were through a mechanical rod device which, on submergence, folded flat on top of the hull. The periscope was 2 in in diameter and only had a single eyepiece.

The armament of these boats lay in the side cargoes, metal cased two three-ton charges of HE which was secured to the submarine by a threaded bolt. This was released from inside the hull by turning a hand wheel. The craft would manoeuvre close to its target, release its side cargo, which included a timing device, and move away before the charge exploded against the harbour bed and the ship's bottom.

X craft were also fitted with a wet-and-dry compartment which enabled one of the crew, suitably clad with underwater breathing gear and armed with limpet mines, to emerge from the boat and swim to the enemy vessel. The limpet mines attached themselves by magnets, but if the enemy ship's bottom was rather foul, the diver had the dangerous job of scraping away the barnacles to give a surface which the mines would hold.

The method of transport for X craft to the scene of attack was varied. They could be towed to within a few miles by a conventional submarine; they could be suspended underneath a vessel for short ranges; or they could be launched from the deck of a larger submarine or surface vessel. The craft were not particularly stable when under tow and the systems had to be monitored. A 'passage crew' controlled the boat, when under tow.

XE24 is preserved at the Royal Naval Submarine Museum, HMS *Dolphin*.

3 MAIN ENGINE ROOM	9 CONTROL ROOM
4 MAIN ENGINE	10 CREW ACCOMODATION
5 MAIN MOTOR	20 MAIN BALLAST TANK

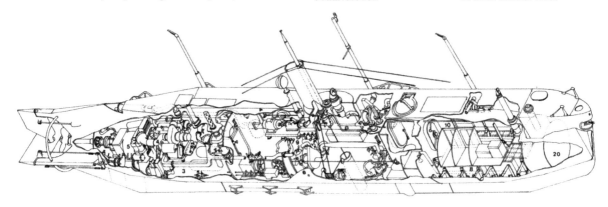

Losses

The following is understood to be accurate from the information available:

X5, X6 and X7 were lost on 22 September 1943 during an attack on the German battleship Tirpitz in Altenfjord, Norway.

X8 was scuttled whilst approaching the Norwegian coast on 17 September 1943.

X10 was scuttled whilst approaching the Norwegian Coast on 3 October 1943.

X9 foundered whilst under tow in the North Sea on 15 October 1943.

X22* collided with the HMS/M Syrtis in the Pentland Firth on 7 February 1944.

XE11 was in collision with a boom defence vessel on 6 March 1945.

XE 22* was in collision in the Pentland Firth with an unknown vessel and lost on 7 February 1944.

*It is uncertain if both X22 and XE 22 were lost; Vickers' Yard List shows XE22 as having been commissioned 31 October 1943 and lost as above. No further details are given.

Stickleback in use as a training boat at Gosport.

X51, later Minnow, when she was operational.

A Welman craft ready for launching complete with warhead.

Specification

Displacement: 4,540 lbs (5,740 lbs with charge)
Dimensions: 17¼ (20½ with charge) x 3½ x 4½ ft
Complement: 1
Propulsion surfaced: Internal combustion engine
submerged: Electric motor
Speed surfaced: 3 knots
Armament: Single charge of 1,200 lbs (of which 600 lbs was HE)

Welfreighter (Marks I–III)
Specification Similar to Welman craft, but designed to have two crew and carry 200 lbs cargo in place of armament.

Class note: The Welman one-man submarine was unique to the Royal Navy. It was invented by Col. Dolphin (co-incidentally the same name as the Royal Navy submarine base at Gosport) and was built at a hotel in Welwyn Garden City, from which it derives its name. The first two craft were built at 'Station IX' between June and August 1942.

The intention was that they would be a weapon against shipping in harbour or, in the Welfreighter mode, used for survey and beach reconnaissance, or to carry stores and weapons to resistance movements in occupied territories.

The craft were strongly built, as is evidenced by a trial in which one was lowered to a depth of 100 ft before imploding. They were, however, slow and had a short range. The HE charge was fixed to the bow and released by a mechanical gear after magnetically attaching to the target.

The Welfreighter building programme commenced in November 1942; trials began at Staines in July 1943 and at Fishguard in March 1944. Six craft were ordered with Shelvoke and Drewry in June 1944. The number was increased to 40, but it is not known if all were completed. Twelve craft were shipped to Australia in mid-1945 (one,

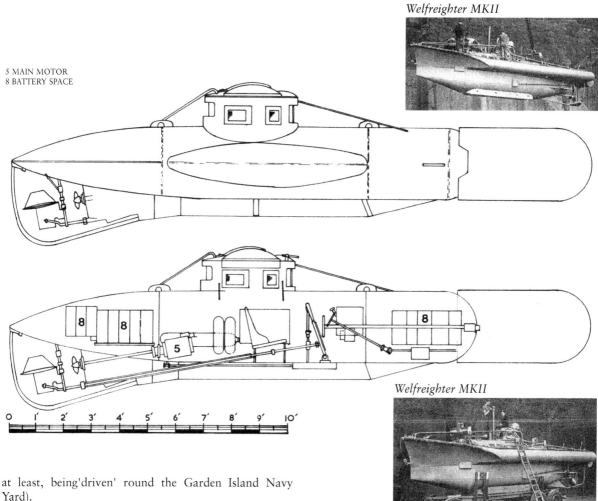

5 MAIN MOTOR
8 BATTERY SPACE

O 1' 2' 3' 4' 5' 6' 7' 8' 9' 10'

Welfreighter MKII

at least, being 'driven' round the Garden Island Navy Yard).

Had the craft been used operationally in Europe they would have been crewed by SOE (Special Operations Executive) personnel.

Only one naval action is recorded in which Welman craft took part. This was an attack by four craft (Nos 45—48) on Bergen harbour on 20—22 November 1943. They were crewed by Lt. J.P. L. Holmes, RN, Lt. V. M. Harris, RNVR, Lt. C. A. Johnson and 2nd Lt. H. Petersen of the Royal Norwegian Army. They were carried to the target area by MTBs, but mistimed their arrival and were forced to spend over a day in hiding near an island outside the harbour where they were seen by local fishermen.

Whether or not for that reason, they found the defences extremely alert when the operation was begun. The first craft was captured and the other three found it impossible to press home their attack despite repeated attempts. The craft were scuttled and the crews made their way ashore where they were aided by the local population. They were finally rescued by MTBs from Shetland on 5 February 1944.

A Welman Mk III about to be launched, complete with warhead, into a Scottish harbour.

	completed	*builder*
N35 U-2326		Deutsche Werft,
(Type XXIII)	1945	Hamburg

Specification

Displacement	surfaced:	232 tons
	submerged:	256 tons
Dimensions:		112 x 9½ x 13 ft
Complement:		14
Propulsion	surfaced:	Diesel engine 580 bhp
	submerged:	Electric motor 600 bhp
		Electric 'creeping' motor 35 shp
Speed	surfaced:	9½ knots
	submerged:	12½ knots;
		'creeping' speed 2 knots
Range	surfaced:	1,400 nm at 9½ knots
	submerged:	175 nm at 4 knots
Armament	Torpedo:	Two 21 in bow tubes

U-2326 shown alongside at Aberdeen in 1945 after surrendering to the HM ships in the North Sea.
W. Cloots

Note the coastal variation of the Type XXI.
N35 as *U-2326* surrendered to the RN and was taken into Aberdeen. Later being evaluated and wearing the White Ensign. Being transferred to the French Navy but was accidentally lost off Toulon on 6th December 1946.

	completed	builder
N41 U-3017		
(Type XXI)	1945	Deschimag, Bremen

Specification

Displacement	surfaced:	1,612 tons
	submerged:	1,819 tons
Dimensions:		251 x 21¾ x 20 ft
Complement:		57
Propulsion	surfaced:	Two diesel engines 4,000 bhp
	submerged:	Two electric motors 5,000 bhp, Two electric 'creeping' motors 226 shp
Speed	surfaced:	15½ knots
	submerged:	16 knots; 'creeping' speed 6 knots
Range	surfaced:	11,150 nm at 12 knots
	submerged:	285 nm at 6 knots
Armament	Gun:	Four 30 mm on two thin mountings (AA)
	Torpedo:	Six 21 in bow tubes 23 reloads
	Mines:	12 with 12 torpedo reloads

HM S/M N41 (ex U-3017) entering the Walney channel (Barrow-in-Furness) en route for Vickers to undergo refurbishment. W. Cloots

Class note: Under Pennant No *N41*, *U-3017* was in commission for evaluation from August to September 1945 and was scrapped in 1949.

Aeneas on builder's trials in the Mersey.

	launched	builder
Achates	1945	HM Dockyard, Devonport
Acheron	1945	HM Dockyard, Chatham
Aeneas, Affray	1945	Cammell Laird
Alaric	1946	Cammell Laird
Alcide, Alderney, Alliance, Ambush	1945	Vickers Armstrong, Barrow-in-Furness
Amphion (later *Anchorite*)	1946	Vickers Armstrong, Barrow-in-Furness
Anchorite (later *Amphion*)	1944	Vickers Armstrong, Barrow-in-Furness
Andrew	1946	Vickers Armstrong, Barrow-in-Furness
Artemis	1946	Scotts
Artful	1947	Scotts
Astute, Auriga, Aurochs	1945	Vickers Armstrong, Barrow-in-Furness

Cancellations: The follwing 28 boats were cancelled. *Abelard, Acasta* (HM Dockyard Portsmouth); *Ace* (HM Dockyard Devonport); *Adept* (HM Dockyard Chatham); *Andromache, Answer, Antaeus, Antagonist, Anzac, Aphrodite, Approach, Arcadian, Ardent, Argosy* (Vickers Armstrong, Barrow-in-Furness); *Admirable, Adversary, Asperity, Austere, Awake, Aztec* (Vickers Armstrong, Newcastle upon Tyne); *Azgard, Assurance, Astarte* (Scotts); *Agate, Aggressor, Agile, Aladdin, Alcestis* (Cammell Laird)

Specification

Displacement	surfaced:	1,385 tons
	submerged:	1,620 tons
Dimensions:		281½ x 22¼ x 17 ft
Complement:		60
Propulsion	surfaced:	Two diesels engines 4,300 hp
	submerged:	Two electric motors 1,250 hp
Speed	surfaced:	18 knots
	submerged:	8 knots;
Fuel	capacity:	300 tons
Armament	Gun:	One 4 in, one 20 mm
	Torpedo:	Ten 21 in tubes; four internal and two external in the bow; two internal and two external in the stern
	Mines:	20 or 26
Range		10,500 nm at 11 knots

A Class submarine's in various stages of completion at Vickers yard.

Astute after her first refit showing all the wartime innovations.

Class notes: The first boat of this class, *Amphion*, was a little unstable therefore a bow buoyancy tank was fitted. This Class was intended for long-range patrol work, particularly in the war against the Japanese, but the majority of the boats were completed after the cessation of hostilities.

Losses

Affray failed to surface in the English Channel on 17 April 1951.

Artemis was inadvertantly flooded when alongside at *Dolphin* jetty on the 1 July 1971 being later raised and paid off.

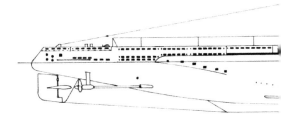

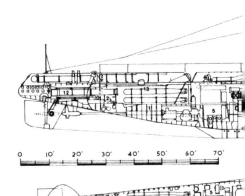

1 TRIMMING TANK	15 FORWARD TORPEDO TUBES
2 STEERING GEAR COMPARTMENT	16 FORWARD TORPEDO STOWAGE
3 MAIN ENGINE ROOM	17 FUEL TANKS
4 MAIN ENGINE	19 RADIO ROOM
5 MAIN MOTOR	20 MAIN BALLAST TANK
8 BATTERY SPACE	23 'Q' TANK
9 CONTROL ROOM	25 SEARCH PERISCOPE
10 CREW ACCOMMODATION	26 ATTACK PERISCOPE
11 WARD ROOM	28 RADAR MAST
12 AFTER TORPEDO TUBES	29 4 in GUN
13 AFTER TORPEDO STOWAGE	

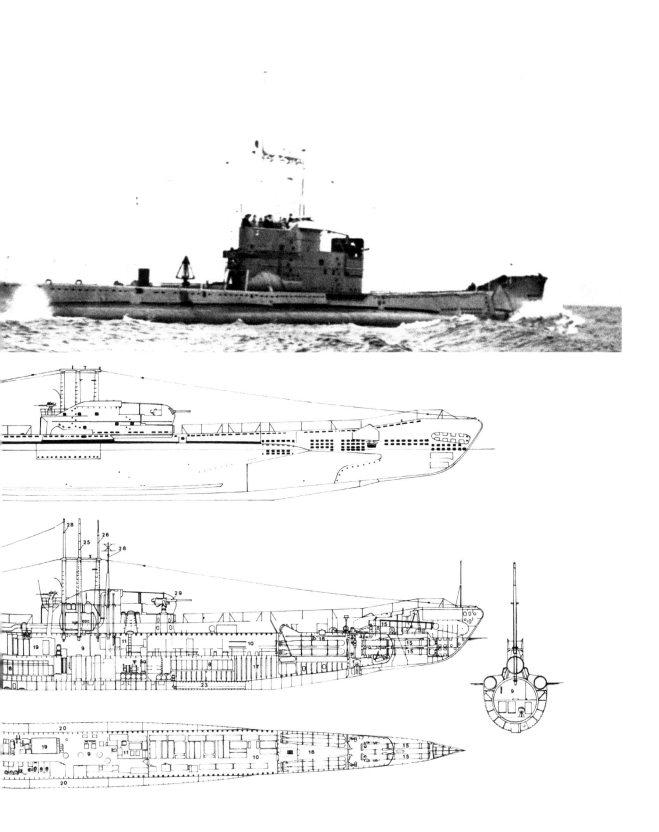

Grampus on builder's trials (as she is wearing the Red Ensign). The bollards fore and aft are retractable.

	commenced	launched	builder
Cachalot	1955	1959	Scotts
Finwhale	1956	1960	Cammell Laird
Grampus	1955	1958	Cammell Laird
Narwhal	1956	1959	Vickers Armstrong Barrow-in-Furness
Porpoise	1954	1958	Vickers Armstrong Barrow-in-Furness
Rorqual	1955	1958	Vickers Armstrong Barrow-in-Furness
Sealion	1958	1961	Cammell Laird
Walrus	1958	1961	Scotts

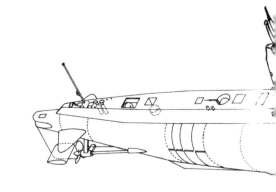

Specification

Displacement	surfaced:	2,030 tons
	submerged:	2,405 tons
Dimensions:		241 bp x 26½ x 18 ft
Complement:		71
Propulsion	surfaced:	Two diesel engines 3,680 bhp
	submerged:	Two electric motors 6,000 shp
Speed	surfaced:	12 knots
	submerged:	17 knots
Range		9,000 nm at 12 knots
Armament	Torpedo:	Eight 21 in tubes, six bow, two stern*, 30 reloads

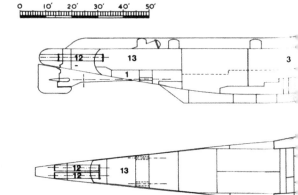

*In some boats the stern tubes were modified to fire 12¾ in torpedoes.

Class note: This was the first major Class to be built for the Royal Navy after World War II. The boats were substantially remodelled in structure and outline from the A and T Classes.

Armament note: From this Class, with the exception of a small number of boats that carried a gun during the period of the Indonesian confrontation, deck guns were no longer mounted. A deck gun in kit form with portable mountings may be stowed in the hull.

This class, and some of the later 'A' Class, incorporated the 'Snort' underwater breathing system. The *Porpoise* and *Oberon* Classes are probably the most efficient conventional powered submarines in the world today. They are noted for their near-silent running. A maximum diving depth of 1,000 ft is understood to be possible.

1 TRIMMING TANK	15 FORWARD TORPEDO TUBES
3 MAIN ENGINE ROOM	16 FORWARD TORPEDO STOWAGE
8 BATTERY SPACE	24 'SNORT' MAST
9 CONTROL ROOM	25 SEARCH PERISCOPE
10 AFTER TORPEDO TUBES	26 ATTACK PERISCOPE
12 AFTER TORPEDO TUBES	27 W/T MAST
13 AFTER TORPEDO STOWAGE	28 RADAR MAST

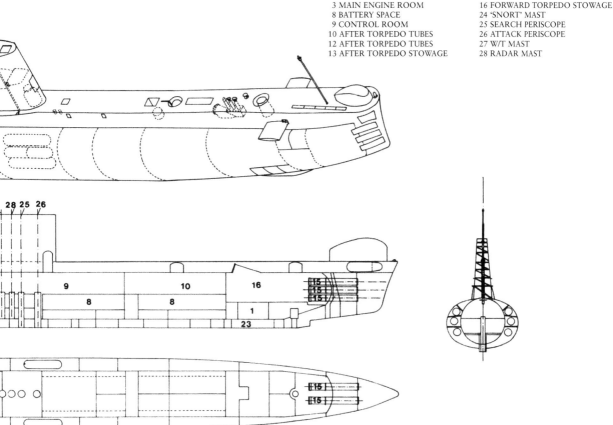

Finwhale on builder's trials in the Clyde.

Sealion prepares to dive into the sunset.

Meteorite at speed, clearly showing the effect of her HTP power system.

	launched	builder
Meteorite	c. 1943	Blohm and Voss,
(ex *U-1407*)		Hamburg

Specification

Displacement	surfaced:	312 tons
	submerged:	357 tons
Dimensions:		136 x 11¼ x 14 ft
Complement:		19
Propulsion	surfaced:	Diesel engine 210 bhp
		Walther HTP turbine
		2,500 shp
	submerged:	Electric motor 77 bhp
Speed	surfaced:	Diesel power 8½ knots;
		turbine 20 knots
	submerged:	5 knots (turbine 20 knots)
Range	surfaced:	Diesel power 3,000 nm at
		8 knots, turbine 115 nm
		20 knots
	submerged:	40 nm at 4½ knots
Armament	Torpedo:	Two 21 in bow tubes,
		four reloads

Note: This boat was found scuttled at Cuxhaven by RN Occupation forces. She was raised in May 1945 for evaluation of the Walther HTP turbine (see below). Vickers were given the task of carrying out trials, the results of which were sufficiently encouraging for the Admiralty to order building of the EX Class.
Meteorite was broken up in 1950.
The Walther Turbine High Test Peroxide system was an advanced experimental means of submarine propulsion developed by the German Navy and first tested in the 80-ton *V80* in 1940. Trials were successful and the HTP system was planned for *V-300*, later *U-791*. This was not carried out, but the system was added to a number of Type VII boats then being built.
The principle of the HTP system was a closed-circuit turbine powered by gas independent of the external atmosphere. The gas was generated from the decomposition in water of concentrated hydrogen peroxide (Penhydral or Ingolin) which produced a hot gas at very high pressure. Fuel consumption was high and the compound unstable.

U-1407 after being raised at Cuxhaven.

Explorer leaving Vickers yard for trials.

	launched	completed	builder
Explorer	1954	1956	Vickers Armstrong, Barrow-in-Furness
Excalibur	1955	1958	Vickers Armstrong, Barrow-in-Furness

Specification

Displacement surfaced: 780 tons
submerged: 1,000 tons
Dimensions: 225½ x 15½ x 11 ft
Complement: *Explorer* 49, *Excalibur* 41
Propulsion: These submarines were unique in having three differing power systems: diesel engines, electric motors, and steam turbines driven by heat from HTP fuel reaction
Speed surfaced: 15 knots
submerged: 30 knots;
Armament: Nil

Class note: These boats were built as experimental submarines for full-scale investigation and testing of hydrogen peroxide fuel. This provided superior power to conventional machinery and was practically noiseless. The experiments continued until 1968 (*Excalibur* was scrapped in 1970) but the fuel compound proved to be so unstable that, as in the early A and B Classes with their petrol engines, the fuel was more dangerous to the boat than the benefits accrued. The idea of hydrogen peroxide power came from investigations and tests into its use by the German Navy (see p. 105). The system was evaluated by the Admiralty in great depth as is evidenced by the building of these two submarines.

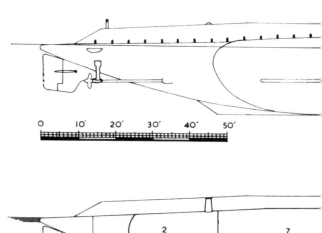

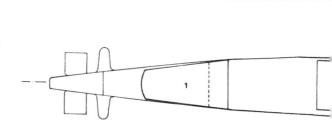

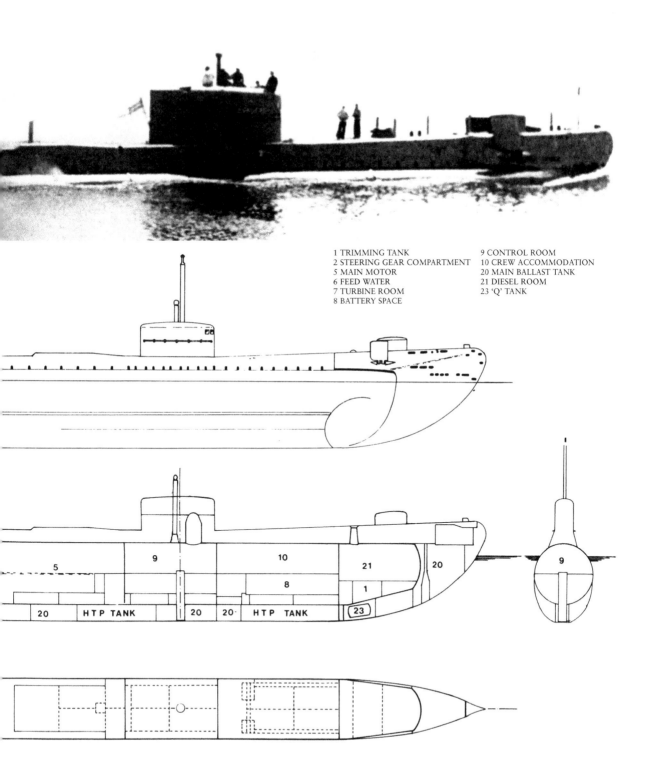

1 TRIMMING TANK
2 STEERING GEAR COMPARTMENT
5 MAIN MOTOR
6 FEED WATER
7 TURBINE ROOM
8 BATTERY SPACE

9 CONTROL ROOM
10 CREW ACCOMMODATION
20 MAIN BALLAST TANK
21 DIESEL ROOM
23 'Q' TANK

	commenced	completed	builder
Oberon	1957	1961	HM Dockyard, Chatham
Ocelot	1960	1964	HM Dockyard, Chatham
Odin	1959	1962	Cammell Laird
Olympus	1960	1962	Vickers Armstrong, Barrow-in-Furness
Onslaught	1959	1962	HM Dockyard, Chatham
Onyx (II)	1964	1967	Cammell Laird
Opossum	1961	1964	Cammell Laird
Opportune	1961	1964	Scotts
Oracle	1960	1963	Cammell Laird
Orpheus	1959	1962	Vickers Armstrong, Barrow-in-Furness
Osiris	1962	1964	Vickers Armstrong, Barrow-in-Furness
Otter	1960	1962	Scotts
Otus	1961	1963	Scotts

HMS Osiris

Specification

Displacement	surfaced:	2,030 tons
	submerged:	2,410 tons
Dimensions:		295¼ x 26½ x 18 ft
Complement:		68
Propulsion	surfaced:	Two diesel engines 3,680 bhp
	submerged:	Two electric motors 6,000 shp
Speed	surfaced:	12 knots
	submerged:	17 knots
Range:		9,000 nm at 12 knots
Armament	Torpedo:	Eight 21 in: six bow and two stern tubes*, 24 reloads

*In some boats the stern tubes were modified to fire 12¾ in torpedoes

Class note: Onyx 1 was sold to Canada after commissioning and renamed Ojibwa. This Class followed a similar design to the Porpoise Class, but with differences in the frames of the pressure hull. Parts of the conning tower were constructed of plastic or glass fibre—it has been reported that some elderly submariners 'found it strange to see the sun shining through the conning tower for a change'.* The conning tower of Orpheus is constructed of aluminium.

Like the Porpoise Class, this Class is said to be able to submerge to 1,000 ft.

* Warships of the Royal Navy, 1979.

Odin moving smoothly in a calm sea.

Dreadnought nearly awash. An early photograph, as she is wearing the Red Ensign and pennant numbers are no longer painted on the conning tower.

	launched	completed	builder
Dreadnought	1960	1963	Vickers Armstrong, Barrow-in-Furness

Specification

Displacement	surfaced:	3,500 tons
	submerged:	4,000 tons
Dimensions:		256¾ bp x 32¼ x 26 ft
Complement:		88
Propulsion	surfaced:	Geared steam turbines 15,000 shp
	submerged:	powered from pressurised water-cooled nuclear reactor
Speed	submerged:	Better than 28 knots
Range:		100,000 nm (approx)
Armament	Torpedo:	Six 21 in bow tubes

Class note: This submarine in much of her design was similar to the *Skipjack* Class of the US Navy. The US government authorising the supply of reactor, propulsion plant and the requisite design know-how, the hull being very largely the work of Admiralty and Vickers designers and constructors. This is a 'one-boat' Class and is the first true nuclear submarine to be built for the Royal Navy. She was taken out of commission in 1982. She was the first British submarine to surface under the ice at the North Pole (in 1971).

The slim silhouette of Dreadnought's conning tower.

The name *Dreadnought* carries twelve Battle Honours from Armada (1588) to Trafalgar (1805).

Nuclear power gives a number of advantages, including high speed and high power, fresh water as required, no danger under depth charge attack from external fuel tanks, and no limit to time submerged by reason of lack of fresh air.

Dreadnought with her hydroplanes angled upward, their position when not in use.

Warspite on trials. Very similar to Dreadnought in appearance.

	commenced	*completed*	*builder*
Valiant	1962	1966	Vickers Shipbuilders, Barrow-in-Furness
Warspite	1963	1967	Vickers Shipbuilders, Barrow-in-Furness

Specification

Displacement	surfaced:	3,500 tons
	submerged:	4,500 tons
Dimensions:		285 x 33¼ x 27 ft
Complement:		103
Propulsion:	Geared steam turbine to one shaft powered by single water-cooled nuclear reactor 15,000 shp	
Speed	submerged:	Better than 28 knots
Range:		80,000 nm (approx)
Armament	Torpedo:	Six 21 in bow tubes; 26 reloads

Class note: A recurring problem in these boats (and in similar Classes in the US Navy) was hairline cracks in the welding which were to very fine tolerances. New welding techniques were developed to overcome the difficulty but frequent dry docking was necessary.

Valiant completed the record submerged voyage of 12,000 nm from Singapore to UK in April 1967. The voyage took 28 days.

Armament note: In 1980 the Class was retrofitted with the Harpoon missile sytem.

Valiant, sister to Warspite, digging in her bows.

Repulse in Plymouth Sound. The design of the hydroplanes should be compared with those in other nuclear powered submarines.

	commenced	completed	builder
Resolution	1964	1967	Vickers Shipbuilders, Barrow-in-Furness
Repulse	1965	1968	Vickers Shipbuilders, Barrow-in-Furness
Renown	1964	1968	Cammell Laird
Revenge	1965	1969	Cammell Laird

One further boat was planned but construction not commenced

Specification

Displacement	surfaced:	7,500 tons
	submerged:	8,400 tons
Dimensions:		360 bp x 33 x 30 ft
Complement:		143 (see Class note)
Propulsion:		Geared steam turbine powered by single pressurised water-cooled nuclear reactor
Speed	submerged:	Better than 25 knots
Range:		100,000 nm (approx)
Armament	Torpedo:	Six 21 in bow tubes
	Missiles:	Sixteen Polaris A3 (see Armament note)

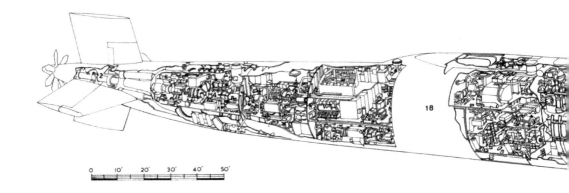

0   10'   20'   30'   40'   50'

Class note: Following the precedent set by the US Navy, these Polaris armed submarines are used as the UK nuclear deterrent because of the vulnerability of the manned bomber to anti-aircraft attack and because the land forces do not possess a strategic nuclear weapon.

These boats normally carry out a two month patrol before returning for a short service. As this imposes a considerable strain on one crew, two are attached to each boat (known as the Port and Starboard crews) which alternate after each patrol. The seagoing limitations of earlier submarines are thus transferred from the boats to the crews.

A new Class has been proposed to replace the Resolution Class. It is planned that there will be four boats to be built by Vickers Shipbuilding and Engineering Ltd of which the first is to be laid down in 1986 for commissioning in 1993. Displacement is planned to be 14,680 tons; propulsion to be from a pressurised water reactor system The boats would have a refit interval of seven years. They would be armed with 16 Trident D5 missiles, with a range of 6,000 nm and each missile would carry 14 independently targeted warheads.

Armament note: The Polaris missiles each carry three Chevaline (Chevaline means 'mountain goat') independently targeted warheads.

Resolution from the stern, giving a good idea of her bulk.

2 STEERING GEAR COMPARTMENT
3 MAIN ENGINE ROOM
9 CONTROL ROOM
10 CREW ACCOMMODATION
11 WARD ROOM

24 'SNORT' MAST
25 SEARCH PERISCOPE
26 ATTACK PERISCOPE
28 RADAR MAST
31 SONAR ROOM

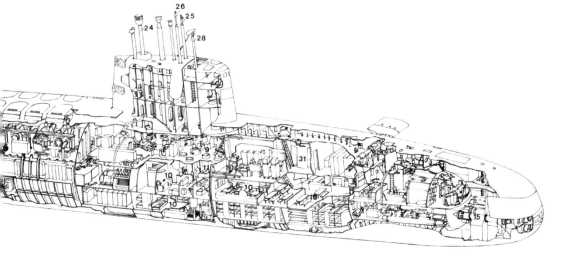

Churchill on trials.

Specification

	commenced	completed	builder
Churchill	1967	1970	Vickers Shipbuilders, Barrow-in-Furness
Conqueror	1967	1971	Cammell Laird
Courageous	1968	1971	Vickers Shipbuilders, Barrow-in-Furness

Specification

Displacement	surfaced:	3,500 tons
	submerged:	4,500 tons
Dimensions:		285 x 33¼ x 27 ft
Complement:		103
Propulsion:	Geared steam turbine to one shaft powered by single pressurised water-cooled nuclear reactor	
Speed	submerged:	Better than 28 knots
Range:		80,000 nm (approx)
Armament	Torpedo:	Six 21 in bow tubes; 26 reloads (see Armament note)

Class note: This was to have been part of the Valiant Class but, by Defence Council instruction, August 1979, it was decided to form a new Class.

Conqueror was one of the Royal Navy submarines involved in the Falklands conflict and sank the Argentine cruiser *General Belgrano* with two Mk 8 torpedoes on 2 May 1982.

Armament note: Rapid torpedo reloading equipment allows reloading in 15 seconds. In 1980 the Class was retrofitted with Harpoon missile system.

Conqueror, showing the speed and power with which she is being propelled and the wave formation created by her hull form.

Launch photograph of Courageous showing her whale-shaped hull.

Swiftsure cruising off the Scottish coast.

	commenced	completed	builder
Sovereign	1970	1974	The whole Class
Superb	1972	1976	built by
Sceptre	1973	1978	Vickers Shipbuilding,
Spartan	1976	1979	Barrow-in-Furness
Splendid (ex *Severn*)			
	1977	1981	
Swiftsure	1969	1973	

Class note: This Class is similar to the Valiant Class but has a shorter hull. The hydroplanes are further forward and the Class has deeper diving capability.

Armament note: Fast reloading capability enables torpedoes to be loaded in 15 seconds. In 1980 the Class was fitted with the Harpoon missile system.

Specification

Displacement	surfaced:	4,000 tons
	submerged:	4,500 tons
Dimensions:		272 x 32¼ x 27 ft
Complement:		97
Propulsion:		Geared steam turbine powered by single pressurised water-cooled nuclear reactor 15,000 shp
		Diesel engine 4,000 hp (auxiliary)
Speed		submerged: Better than 30 knots
Range:		Approx 75,000 nm
Armament	Torpedo:	Five 21 in bow tubes (20 reloads)

Sceptre exercising with a Wessex helicopter.

S/M	commenced	completed	builder
Talent	1986	1989	Vickers Shipbuilding, Barrow-in-Furness
Tireless	1982	1985	Vickers Shipbuilding, Barrow-in-Furness
Torbay	1982	1987	Vickers Shipbuilding, Barrow-in-Furness
Trafalgar	1979	1983	Vickers Shipbuilding, Barrow-in-Furness
Trenchant	1984	1988	Vickers Shipbuilding, Barrow-in-Furness
Triumph	1986	1991	Vickers Shipbuilding, Barrow-in-Furness
Turbulent	1980	1984	Vickers Shipbuilding, Barrow-in-Furness

Specification

Displacement	surfaced:	4,700 tons
	submerged:	5,208 tons
Dimensions:		280 x 32 x 26¾ ft
Complement:		130
Propulsion:		Geared steam turbine to one shaft powered by a pressurised water-cooled reactor giving 18,000 shp
Speed	submerged:	30 knots
	radius:	85 days
Diving Depth:		Better than 1000 ft
Armament	Torpedo:	Five 21 in bow tubes for Mk 24 torpedoes, 20 are carried. Also Sub-Harpoon Inter alia.

Class note: This Class is to be fitted with noise-insulating tiles on the hull to reduce the amount of noise emitted, one of the principal means of submarine detection. The Class will thus be much quieter than the Swiftsure Class. Reactor endurance is intended to be two-three years though in peacetime **patrols will probably be limited to two months.**

Armament note: The torpedo armament includes Tigerfish wire-guided homing torpedoes in addition to the unguided type.

Notes: The hull is covered with anechoic tiles to reduce radiation and reflected noise. Very similar to boats of the *Swiftsure* Class but reputed to be much quieter. A follow-on class has been the subject of a design study and is known as Type SSN 20.

The launch of Trafalgar. The angular metal cover on the bows is a security measure to conceal the weapon exits.

HM S/M	commenced	completed	builder
Vanguard	1986	1993	Vickers Armstrong, Barrow-in-Furness
Venerable (later *Vigilant*)	1990	1996	Vickers Armstrong, Barrow-in-Furness
Vengeance (later *Valiant*)	1992	1999	Vickers Armstrong, Barrow-in-Furness
Victorious	1987	1995	Vickers Armstrong, Barrow-in-Furness

Specification

Displacement	surfaced:	14,680 tons
	submerged:	15,850 tons
Dimensions:		492 x 42 x 38 ft
Complement:		130
Machinery:		Geared steam turbine powered by a single pressurised water cooled reactor 22,500 shp
Speed	submerged:	Better than 25 knots
Armament	Missiles	16 Trident D5 II each with 14 independantly targeted warheads.
	Torpedo:	Four 21 in bow tubes for Mk 24 torpedoes, 20 are carried. Also Sub-Harpoon inter alia.

Notes: The missile compartment of the hull is based on that of the *USS Ohio* Class but with 8 less ICBM's. The hulls will be covered with anechoic tiles. To replace boats of the *Resolution* Class.

A Vanguard Class ICBM boat at speed on the surface.

HM S/M	CNS	commenced	completed	builder
Unicorn	(later Windsor)	1990	1993	Cammell Laird
Unseen	(later Victoria)	1987	1990	Cammell Laird
Upholder	(later Chicoutmi)	1983	1990	Vickers Armstrong, Barrow-in-Furness
Ursula	(later Corner Brook)	1989	1992	Cammell Laird

Specification

Displacement	surfaced:	2,185 tons
	submerged:	2,400 tons
Dimensions:		230 x 25 x 27½ ft
Complement:		44
Propulsion:		Diesel electric with two diesel engines 4035 BHP
		Electric motors giving 5,000 kw
Speed	surfaced:	12 knots
	submerged:	20 knots
Fuel Capacity:		200 tons diesel oil.

Range:		10,000 nm at snorting depth
Diving Depth:		Better than 500 ft
Armament	Torpedo:	Six 21 in tubes for Mk 24 torpedoes, 18 are carried. Also Sub-Harpoon inter alia, (able to lay mines).

Notes: This design of submarine using diesel propulsion is the first since the *Oberon* Class of 1961–67 and *Onyx* (II) completed in the latter year. All this Class, laid up in 1994 but sold to Canada in 1998 then refitted at Barrow-in-Furness.

HMS Unicorn entering harbour looking in good trim.

HMS Upholder on a serene sea and flying the White Ensign.

	commenced	rolled-out	builder
Astute	2001	2007	BAE Systems Vickers Yd Barrow-in-Furness (All of this Class)
Ambush	2003	There is a delay	
Artful	2003	on build	

Specification

Displacement	surfaced:	6,690 tons
	submerged:	7,800 tons
Dimensions:		318¼ x 37 x 32¾ ft
Complement:		98 (with 12 spare berths)
Propulsion:		Geared steam turbine powered from a PWR 2 Reactor producing 27,000 shp with two auxiliary diesel alternators and an auxiliary propulsor
Speed		submerged: 29 knots
Range:		85,000 nm approximately
Armament:		Six 21 in bow tubes to discharge mines, Tomahawk surface to surface missiles and Spearfish torpedoes.

Notes: The type H reactor is good for 25+ years and the forward hydroplanes do not retract. The wet and dry compartment has a capacity for 6 persons.

The largest of our SSN's to date although delivery per boat is very much slower than expected.

APPENDIX A: Royal Navy submarines lost in peacetime

Holland No 5	K15
A3	L9
A4	L23
A7	L24
A8	L55
B2	M1
C11	Poseidon
C14	Affray
G11	Sidon
H4	Sportsman
H29	Safari
H42	Thetis
H43	Truculent
H47	Truant
K5	

Causes of loss:

Collision	12
Sea hazard	6
Accident	2
Gunfire	1
Other cause	9
Total	31

APPENDIX B: Royal Navy submarines lost 1914–18

A1	E5	E34
A2	E6	E36
B10	E7	E37
C3	E8	E47
C26	E9	E49
C27	E10	E50
C29	E13	G7
C31	E14	G8
C32	E15	G9
C33	E16	H3
C34	E17	H5
C35	E18	H6
D2	E19	H10
D3	E20	J6
D5	E22	K1
D6	E24	K4
E1	E26	K17
E3	E30	L10

Causes of loss:

Surface action	3
Submarine	4
Mined	4
Destroyed to avoid capture	9
Blockship	1*
Collision	4
Wrecked	4
Accident	4
Unknown	21
Total	54

*Blown up at Zeebrugge Mole.

A3 running on the surface

U-Boat	Date	Location	HM S/M
U-6	15.9.15	North Sea	E16
U-23	20.7.17	North Sea	C27 & HMS Princess Louise
U-40	23.6.15	off Girdle Ness	C24 & HM trawler
U-45	12.9.17	off Malin Head	D7
U-51	14.7.16	Heligoland Bight	H5
U-78	28.10.18	North Sea	G2
U-154	11.5.18	off Cape St Vincent	E35
UB-16	10.5.18	North Sea	E34
UB-52	23.5.18	in the Adriatic	H4
UB-72	12.5.18	English Channel	D2
UB-90	16.10.18	off the Norwegian coast	L12
UC-10	6.7.15	off Schouwen Light Vessel	E54
UC-43	10.3.17	off Muckle Flugga Light House	G13
UC-62	10.17	off Lowestoft	E45
UC-63	1.11.17	Straits of Dover	E52
UC-65	3.11.17	Straits of Dover	C15
UC-68	5.4.17	North Sea	C7
UC-79	19.10.17	North Sea	E45

B1 (ex *Sunfish*)
Cachalot
Grampus
H31
H49
Jastrzab
Narwal
Odin
Olympus
Orpheus
Oswald
Oxley
P32
P33
P36
P38
P39
P48
P222
P311
P514
P715 (ex *Graph*)
Pandora
Parthian
Perseus

Phoenix
Porpoise
Rainbow
Regent
Regulus
Sahib
Salmon
Saracen
Sea Horse
Shark
Sickle
Simoom
Snapper
Spearfish
Splendid
Starfish
Sterlet
Stonehenge
Stratagem
Swordfish
Syrtis
Talisman
Tarpon
Tempest
Tetrarch

Thames
Thistle
Thorn
Thunderbolt
Tigris
Traveller
Triad
Triton
Triumph
Trooper
Turbulent
Umpire
Unbeaten
Undaunted
Undine
Union
Unique
Unity
Untamed*
Upholder
Uredd (ex *P41*)
Urge
Usk
Usurper
Utmost
Vandal
X Craft: 5–10,22

*Subsequently salvaged and renamed *Vitality*.

Causes of Loss RN Submarines and X-craft, 1939–45

	Mined	Aircraft	Submarine	Surface action	Rammed	Enemy action cause unknown	Collision	Accident	Unknown	Own Forces	Wrecked
S/M	23	5	4	13	2	–	1	5	20	2	1
XC	–	–	–	–	–	6	1	–	–	–	–

Totals: S/M 76
XC 7
83

APPENDIX E: German U-Boats sunk by RN submarines in World War II

U-Boat	Date	Location	HM S/M
U-1	16.4.40	North Sea	Porpoise
U-36	4.12.39	North Sea	Salmon
U-51	20.8.40	Bay of Biscay	Cachalot
U-54	12.4.40	North Sea	Salmon
U-301	21.1.43	off Corsica	Sahib
U-303	21.5.43	off Toulon	Sickle
U-308	4.6.43	north of the Faeroes	Truculent
U-335	3.8.42	north of the Faeroes	Saracen
U-374	12.1.42	off Catania	Unbeaten
U-431	30.10.43	off Toulon	Ultimatum
U-486	12.4.45	north-west of Bergen	Tapir
U-644	7.4.43	north-west of Narvik	Tuna
U-771	11.11.44	off the Lofoten Islands	Venturer
U-859	10.10.44	Straits of Malacca	Trenchant
U-987	15.6.44	west of Narvik	Satyr
U-864	9.2.45	west of Bergen	Venturer

Italian U-Boats sunk by RN submarines in World War II

U-Boat	Date	Location	HM S/M
Acciaio	13.7.43	Straits of Messina	Unruly
Ammiraglio Enrico Millo	14.3.42	off Calabria	Ultimatum
Ammiraglio St Bon	5.1.42	off Sicily	Upholder
Diamante	20.6.40	off Torbuk	Parthian
Graneto	9.11.42	off north-west Sicily	Saracen
Guglielmotti	17.3.42	off Sicily	Unbeaten
Jantina	5.7.41	off north coast of Egypt	Torbay
Medusa	30.1.42	Adriatic	Thorn
Michele Bianchi	7.10.41	Adriatic	Severn
Pier Capponi	31.3.41	off Sicily	Rorqual
Pietro Micca	29.7.43	Straits of Taranto	Trooper
Porfido	6.12.42	South of Sardinia	Tigris
Remo	15.7.43	Gulf of Taranto	United
Salpoa	27.1.41	off north coast of Egypt	Triumph
Capitano Tarantina	15.12.40	Bay of Biscay	Thunderbolt
Tricheco	18.3.42	Adriatic	Upholder
U-IT23 (ex Reginaldo Giuliani)	14.2.44	Malacca Straits	Tally Ho
Velella	7.9.43	Gulf of Salerno	Shakespeare

A German U-Boat under attack in World War II.

Japanese U-Boats sunk by RN submarines
in World War II

U-Boat	Date	Location	HM S/M
I-34	13.11.43	Straits of Malacca	*Taurus*
I-166	17.7.44	off Perang	*Telemachus*

A P P E N D I X F : U-Boats taken over by the Royal Navy for evaluation 1939–49

U-Boat No.	Type	Postwar Career
U-712	VIIC	Scrapped
U-795	XVII	Scrapped
U-926	VIIC	Transferred to Norway 1947 as *Kya*
U-953	VIIC	Broken up 1949
U-1057	VIIC	Transferred to Russia 1946
U-1058	VIIC	Transferred to Russia 1946
U-1064	VIIC	Transferred to Russia *S81*
U-1105	VIIC 41/42	Later HM S/M *N16*
U-1171	VIIC 41/42	Later HM S/M *N19*
U-1202	VIIC 41/42	Transferred to Norway 1947 as *Kynn*
U-1407	XVIIB	Later HM S/M *Meteorite*
U-2326	XXIII	Later HM S/M *N35* transferred to France 1946
U-2353	XXIII	Later HM S/M *N31* transferred to Russia later
U-2518	XXI	Transferred to France 1946
U-2529	XXI	Later HM S/M *N27* transferred to Russia 1946
U-3017	XXI	Later HM S/M *N41* scrapped 1949
U-3035	XXI	Later HM S/M *N28* transferred to Russia 1946
U-3041	XXI	Later HM S/M *N29* transferred to Russia 1946
U-3515	XXI	Later HM S/M *N30* transferred to Russia 1946
U-4706	XXVI	Transferred to Norway 1948 as *Knerter*

U-1105 had been covered entirely by the Germans with a special rubber coating which it was hoped would absorb the asdic (sonar) pings, thus reducing the chances of detection. The Royal Navy ran this boat for some months in late 1945. It was then handed over to the US Navy, and after further trials was scuttled. Whilst in RN service the boat was nicknamed 'The Black Panther". Another of the boats, number so far unidentified, had a sponge rubber coating around the head of the Snorkel mast. The sponge rubber was painted with an aluminium paint to deaden the radar pulses and so, again, reduce the chance of detection. This boat was nicknamed 'The White Puma'.

U135 with a Royal Navy crew on board shortly after World War I.

The submarine was the only naval vessel built to be armed effectively by one weapon—the torpedo. Twenty-eight years prior to the first Royal Navy submarine, the torpedo boat was designed and built in large numbers to carry the weapon but it has been more successfully employed by the submarine than by any surface vessel.

The torpedo in the Holland Class was 14 in calibre; in the A Class it was increased to 18 in and the D Class of 1908 first carried the 21 in torpedo. This is still the calibre used in nuclear powered submarines. Torpedoes like all other forms of armament, have undergone considerable development over the years. The Tigerfish wire guided torpedo was introduced in 1980 but has had some problems, and in the South Atlantic campaign of 1982 the torpedoes used to sink the Argentine cruiser *General Belgrano* were the rather elderly Mk 8. Type 7525, known as Spearfish which is a further development of the Tigerfish, being announced in 1982 and both are of the heavy long-range type.

For surface use, the deck gun of the submarine varied from a single 3 pdr to a single 12 in, as fitted in the M Class. The most common deck gun for the submarine was the short 4 in mounted forward of the conning tower. This had a nominal muzzle velocity of 2,500 ft/sec and a range of four nm. In later years submarines were equipped with a number of weapons to combat aircraft, ranging from the .303 Lewis gun to the 20 mm Oerlikon, used by every ship in the Fleet. The 40 mm Bofors gun does not appear to have been part of a submarine armament. The 3 in HA/DP weapon, nominally the 12 pdr (sometimes 14 pdr) was also intended to be an anti-aircraft weapon. Their minimal directional equipment for high-level fire made their effectiveness questionable against aircraft.

More recently the missile with a guidance system has been proposed, and the Slam/Blow Pipe two-stage solid-fuel rocket with optical or radio guidance and an HE warhead have been on trial. Polaris was the first intermediate-range ballistic missile (IRBM) developed for launching from a submerged submarine.

Type A1 was first fired successfully from USN S/M *George Washington* on 20 July 1960. It was subsequently developed to Type A3 which is powered by a two-stage solid propellant rocket motor. It has a built-in inertial guidance system which is motivated by geo-ballistic and navigational computers on board the launching submarine. These feed information to the IRBM system until the moment of launch after which it becomes entirely independent.

The missiles are mounted vertically in the submarine. The initial stage of launch is from steam pressure generated in the launch tube by firing a small rocket motor into a water chamber beneath it. After emergence at the surface the missile's own first stage is fired.

The missile is 32¼ ft long and 4½ ft in diameter; the launch weight is 35,000 lbs and the range 2,800 nm. It is armed with the Chevaline system of independently targeted warheads. The Trident system has been designated the successor to Polaris. This intercontinental ballistic missile (ICBM) carries eight independently targetted warheads. Sixteeen missiles are to be mounted in each submarine, giving a total of 128 target options. The warhead on each is to be about 100 kilotons. Trident is to be 34ft long and 6ft 2 in diameter; the launch weight is approx. 36,000 lbs and the missile has a range of 4,350 nm.

Harpoon is a tactical missile system with an effective range of 55—120nm for surface to surface (SSM) or underwater to surface (USM) use. In this configuration the weapon is fired from a torpedo tube conventionally by compressed air, after which it utilises its built-in turbojet and rocket motors. Guidance is radar-programmed/satellite. Harpoon is 15 ft long, weights 1,470 lbs and has a speed of Mach 0.9. It carries a 500 lb HE or thermonuclear warhead and was test launched from HM S/M *Churchill* in April 1980.

A Spearfish 21 in torpedo.

A Tigerfish 21 in wire guided torpedo. The photograph clearly shows the wire coil in its guard behind the contra-rotating propellers.

A Tigerfish 21 in torpedo being taken on board HM S/M Conqueror.

APPENDIX H: Submarine builders in the
United Kingdom, Canada and the USA

Sir W.G. Armstrong Whitworth & Co Ltd, Newcastle
upon Tyne, Northumberland
William Beardmore & Co Ltd, Dalmuir, Glasgow
Bethlehem Shipbuilding Corporation Ltd, Bethlehem, Pa,
USA also at Fore River Plant, Quincy, Mass, USA, and
Union Iron Works, San Francisco, USA
John Brown & Co Ltd, Clydebank
Cammell Laird & Co Ltd, Birkenhead
Canadian Vickers, Montreal, Canada
William Denny & Brothers, Dumbarton, Strathclyde,
Scotland
HM Dockyard, Chatham, Kent
HM Dockyard, Devonport, Devon
HM Dockyard, Pembroke, Dyfed, Wales
HM Dockyard, Portsmouth, Hampshire
Fairfield Shipbuilding & Engineering Co Ltd, Govan,
Glasgow
Palmers Shipbuilding & Iron Co, Hebburn, Tyne and
Wear
Scotts Shipbuilding & Engineering Co Ltd, Greenock,
Strath-Clyde, Scotland
Swan Hunter & Wigham Richardson Ltd, Wallsend,
Tyne and Wear
J. I. Thornycroft & Co Ltd, Woolston, Hampshire
Vickers Ltd, Barrow-in-Furness, Cumbria
J. Samuel White & Co Ltd, Cowes, Isle of Wight
Yarrow & Co, Scotstoun, Strathclyde, Scotland

BIBLIOGRAPHY

The War at Sea, Captain S. W. Roskill, HMSO
Japanese Warships of World War II, A. J. Watts, lan Allan
Warships of World War 1, H. M. Le Fleming, lan Allan
Jane's Fighting Ships (various editions) Sampson Low &
Marston
Jane's Pocket Book No 8, John E. Moore, Macdonald &
Jane's
Warships of World War II, H. T. Lenton & J. J. Colledge,
Ian Allan
Transactions of the Royal Institution of Naval Architects
(various years), RINA, London
Axis Submarines, A. J. Watts, Macdonald & Jane's
Allied Submarines, A. J. Watts, Macdonald &Jane's
Jane's Pocket Book No 9, Denis Archer, Macdonald &
Jane's
British Warships 1914-1919, F. J. Dittmar & J. J.
Colledge, Ian Allan
Yard Shipbuilding List, Vickers Shipbuilding Group
German Warships of World War II, J. C. Taylor, Ian Allan
Warships of the Royal Navy, Captain J. E. Moore, RN,
Macdonald & Jane's
British Escort Ships, H. T. Lenton, Macdonald & Jane's
*The Development of H.M. Submarines from Holland No
1 (1901) to Porpoise (1930),* A. N. Harrison, Ministry
of Defence.

*HMS Forth, a submarine depot ship in Devonport
dockyard, 1962.*

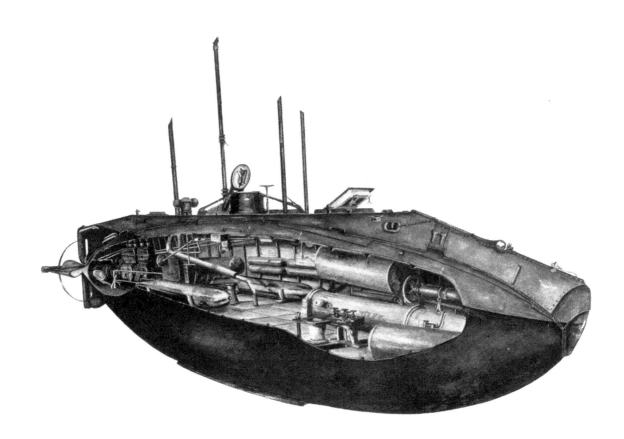

HOLLAND CLASS 1901
THE FIRST ROYAL NAVY SUBMARINE